The Canadian Guide to Protecting Yourself from
Identity Theft and Other Fraud

Be safe!
Connie Bird

The Canadian Guide to Protecting Yourself from Identity Theft and Other Fraud

Graham McWaters and Gary Ford

INSOMNIAC PRESS

Library and Archives Canada Cataloguing in Publication

McWaters, Graham, 1956-   The Canadian guide to protecting yourself from
identity theft and other fraud / Graham McWaters and Gary Ford.

Includes bibliographical references and index. ISBN 978-1-897178-46-1

    1. Identity theft. 2. Identity theft--Canada--Prevention. 3. Fraud. 4. Fraud-
-Canada--Prevention. I. Ford, Gary, 1946- II. Title.
HV6685.C3M39 2007   364.16'30971   C2007-904513-8

The publisher gratefully acknowledges the support of the Department of Canadian
Heritage through the Book Publishing Industry Development Program.

Printed and bound in Canada

Insomniac Press
192 Spadina Avenue, Suite 403
Toronto, Ontario, Canada, M5T 2C2
www.insomniacpress.com

This book is dedicated to all the victims of identity theft and other fraud, who have suffered emotionally and financially.

This book is dedicated to all the consumers, law enforcement agencies, bankers, lenders, mortgage sales forces, mortgage brokers, lawyers, realtors, title insurers, mortgage insurers, appraisers, credit card issuers, Internet service providers, software developers, credit reporting agencies, financial advisors, securities regulators, and Better Business Bureaus that recognize, prevent, stop, and report identity theft and other forms of fraud.

Disclaimer

Contents

Steal Your Home? The Devil You Know, Power of Attorney Fraud, The Devil You Don't Know, Tenant Fraud, Mortgage by an Impostor, The Fictitious Law Firm, Fraud across Canada, Oklahoma Fraud: Valuation Fraud, Condo Parking Space Fraud, Red Flags of Potential Mortgage and Title Fraud, Consequences and Remedies

What Is Investment Fraud? Spam E-Mail Promoting Stocks, Nigerian 419 Spam E-Mail, Phony Websites, Ponzi Schemes, Pyramid Schemes, Advertisements Promoting Investment Opportunities, Boiler Rooms, Red Flags of Potential Investment Fraud, Protect Your Money and Investments

Target Victims and Groups, Recognizing Telephone Fraud, Toll-Free Telephone Number Scams, 900 Scams, Tips for Recognizing Telephone Fraud, Tips for Avoiding Telephone Fraud

Why Fraudsters Target Seniors, Other Factors That Aggravate the Problem, Types of Financial Exploitation of the Elderly, Wired Seniors, Providing Assistance to Senior Fraud Victims, Warning Signs of Fraudulent Behaviour, Avoiding Con-Artist Schemes, What to Do for the Victim

Congratulations! You Won! (Or So You Think), Advance Fee for Loan Schemes, Tips to Avoid Advance Fee for Loan Schemes, Charity Fraud, Faith-Based Investment Scams, Medical Fraud

Introduction

Identity theft and other forms of fraud can happen to you every day during your normal routine. If you have a credit or debit card, you are vulnerable each time you use your card or carry it in your wallet. When you open e-mail, you could be starting the process of relinquishing your confidential and personal information to a complete stranger through a virus. The act of putting your home up for rent or sale can also invite fraudsters into your life, allowing them to steal your home or place a fraudulent mortgage on your title.

Identity theft is an epidemic in North America and is one of the fastest growing crimes. Fraudsters are using many schemes and techniques to try and steal your personal information, your assets, your identity, and your home. These crimes are annoying for the victims and can be very costly, especially when you calculate the time lost trying to repair your credit, replace a credit card, and restore your identity. Lost assets such as money, securities, or your home, may never be replaced in some situations.

The topics covered in this book include: identity theft, debit and credit card fraud, credit reports, Internet and e-mail fraud, mortgage and title fraud, investment fraud, telephone fraud, and fraud against seniors. Seniors are a favourite target of con artists, and with our aging society, we need to be aware of all the things we can do to prevent fraud against this vulnerable group.

This book will assist you in preventing your identity from being taken and knowing what to do if it does happen.

If you are a homeowner, you will want to pay special attention to the chapter on Mortgage and Title Fraud. Each province and territory in Canada has different processes for managing their land title transfers and mortgage registrations as well as remedies for fraudulent activities. We will help you understand the various processes and actions you can take to prevent or repair mortgage and title fraud.

The appendix of the book outlines many useful items such as: an identity theft statement with instructions, contact information for the three Canadian credit reporting agencies, the Better Business Bureaus, and the provincial and territorial securities regulators. We have also listed the many sources and references used in our research for the book. There are a few websites that are extremely useful depending on the topic you wish to explore. We encourage you to surf the Internet; however, do it carefully!

We have included many true stories about identity theft and other fraudulent activities throughout the book. Once you see how fraud can take place, how it affects you, and what to do if it happens, you will be in a better position to prevent it. There are two messages throughout the book: "Protect your personal information and your assets" and "If it sounds too good to be true, it probably is." Let's each do our part in preventing fraud, recognizing it, reporting it, and stopping it.

Chapter 1

Identity Theft

Alicia McAteer was an eighteen-year-old student who had just finished her second year at Kwantlen College in BC when she became a victim of identity theft. As reported in *The Vancouver Sun* on June 24, 2006, Alicia was standing outside a bowling alley in January 2005 when someone stole her purse. She thought it was a prank being played on her by one of her friends at first, but no one saw what happened.

Alicia filed a report that night with the Langley RCMP and started replacing her driver's license, social insurance card, BC health card, and student card. It was an annoyance but not all that taxing, initially. Her biggest worry at the time was the loss of her actual purse and her new cell phone.

In May 2005, she got a call from Mount Seymour saying the snowboard she had rented had been damaged. Alicia doesn't snowboard. In June 2005, a video store called saying she hadn't returned her past-due videos. She didn't have an account with that store. Then, in September 2005, she got a call from the Insurance Corporation of British Columbia (ICBC). They asked why she wasn't responding to the notice they had sent about her accident. They asked her about her blue Oldsmobile. She drove a green Neon and had never been in an accident. The government worker asked if she lived on Wharf Road in Sechelt. "No," she answered, "I live in Surrey." This is when Alicia really began to worry.

Alicia spent several days trying to prove that the person in the Oldsmobile was not her, even though the impostor had her name and her driver's license. She provided the ICBC with a copy of her police report and asked her boss to write a letter as proof of the fact that she was at work at the time of the accident.

An ICBC fraud prevention officer noticed the witness description of the woman driving the car did not match Alicia's eye colour, weight or height. Alicia's file was cleared, though not completely. She then contacted two credit bureaus—Equifax and TransUnion—to place a fraud alert on her credit reports. "I thought I was all done at that point," she said.

In April 2006, just before going on a two-week vacation to Mexico, Alicia got a call from the Vancouver Police Department, who was investigating two fraud complaints. Someone using her name was cashing large counterfeit cheques. They had also used a fraudulent personal cheque to purchase thousands of dollars in stamps. Alicia met with the Vancouver police to set the record straight. A fuzzy piece of video footage on a surveillance camera exonerated her and she left for her vacation.

While in Mexico, Alicia tried to withdraw $20 from a bank machine, but there was no balance left in her bank account even though she had saved up over $700 for the trip. She called her father, who went to the bank and deposited money for her. In his discussion with the bank, her father discovered the withdrawals had taken place locally in Vancouver while Alicia was in Mexico.

Upon Alicia's return, she had to convince the bank that $7,000 in counterfeit cheques were not her doing. When she asked the bank what she was going to do about her money, the bank said she didn't have any. "I went home and cried and freaked out," Alicia recalled. The bank eventually replaced her money.

In the meantime, Alicia setup a new account and a new credit card with the same bank because her old accounts had been linked up to the impostor's Sechelt address. In a mere 24 hours, her new account had been linked up to the fraudster's Sechelt address again because the impostor had the same name and Alicia's social insurance card. Her newly ordered Visa card was also mailed to the Sechelt address.

Fed up, Alicia closed all her accounts and opened a savings account with a credit union but was refused a credit card because she was deemed a credit risk. When she phoned the Vancouver Police Department to report her bank fraud, an officer told her to call the RCMP since it happened in Burnaby. She called and visited the RCMP in Burnaby but had not heard back.

"Once I switched banks, I thought things would be okay," she said. "Then I got a letter from the government. It was a letter saying my license was being prohibited due to these tickets." The letter said she had been charged on April 12, 2006, with speeding and driving contrary to the restrictions on her license. "I flipped out, I absolutely flipped out. It was just one thing after another."

Alicia called the 1-800 number and explained her identity theft situation. She was sent a victim-identification package to fill out and prove through letters from school and her employer (once again) as to where she was during the date of the speeding infraction. When the ICBC received her package, the suspension threat would be put on hold until the police officer who issued the infraction agreed that Alicia wasn't the person driving the speeding car. If the officer didn't believe her, Alicia's next option would be to go to court.

Alicia was frustrated. She felt her case should be easily solved since she had been told that the bank had a good surveillance tape of the impersonator, ICBC had a name, and Vancouver police had a description. In addition, the Sechelt RCMP phoned to tell her that an officer had stopped the woman for shoplifting baby food but didn't make the connection to the fraud complaints and let her go. A Canada Post employee in West Vancouver called the police after the woman tried to use a personal cheque to buy more stamps. The employee had asked for ID because Canada Post had flagged Alicia's name. The woman said she would get her ID from the car and never returned.

"I don't understand why nothing can be done," Alicia said. "I don't see how she is getting away with it. How can she go into banks and do thousands of dollars in fraud and crash cars and still get away with it?"

The ICBC fraud officer contacted police with her observation that the woman involved in the car accident did not look like Alicia. She said it is up to the police to lay criminal charges.

Sgt. Ken Athans, head of the Vancouver Police Identity Theft Task Force, was not familiar with Alicia's file. That's because his highly successful task force targets large groups of people who work together across the Lower Mainland to pull off organized and very lucrative identity thefts. He had sympathy for Alicia. In an ideal world, there would be enough manpower and cooperation between agencies and police forces to solve a case like hers. Identity theft cases are complicated and often involve more than one jurisdiction. No one agency may step up to take responsibility for individuals like Alicia.

The ICBC will not allow anyone, including victims of identity theft, to get a new driver's license number because a person's driving record stays with them for life. And it wouldn't stop the impostor who has her original license, which doesn't expire until 2008. The ICBC flags a driver's license as stolen so fraud staff or police are alerted about any activity involving the license. The ICBC is introducing a better system that ensures that once a flagged license comes in for a transaction such as a renewal, the license holder will have to answer some personal questions about the person whose name is on the card.

Alicia McAteer, now twenty, has learned her lesson and only carries a minimal amount of identification in her wallet. But she is still terrified her impersonator will continue to haunt her until police make an arrest, and there is no indication that will happen any time soon.

"It's just the most frustrating feeling in the entire world knowing everyone is blaming you for something bad you haven't done," she said. "It's been hell."

It Can Happen to You

When you think of theft, what comes to mind? Is it having your car stolen or someone breaking into your house, stealing your jewellery, television, or stereo? Today, of far greater concern is the theft of your identity—the stealing of your good name and having bad things happen to it.

Open your purse or wallet right now. Are you carrying your birth certificate? Are you carrying your social insurance card? Why? Do you need to provide these crucial identification documents to someone every day? Do you leave your purse in your unlocked desk at work or in the grocery store shopping cart unattended even briefly? Do you leave your wallet in your suit jacket hanging up in your office at work or in the glove compartment of your car?

Here's what could happen: An identity thief takes over your identity and takes over all your financial accounts. With your identification, with their picture now embedded on it, they can open new accounts; transfer bank balances; and apply for loans, credit cards, and mortgages. The thief may purchase big-ticket items or purchase a cell phone in your name. Basically, the identity thief takes over being you in the world, but without the financial responsibility to repay the debts they acquired in your good name.

You will be left to clean up the mess, even though you may not be stuck with paying the imposter's bills, you are often left with a bad credit report and must spend months and even years regaining your financial health. In the meantime, you will have difficulty getting credit, obtaining loans, renting apartments, and even getting hired. Victims of identity theft may find little help from the authorities as they attempt to untangle the web of deception that has allowed another person to impersonate them.

What Is Identity Theft and Identity Fraud?

Identity theft is the stealing of personal information of an actual person. This person may be either living or dead. The thief uses the stolen or fraudulently obtained personal information (or forged or stolen identity documents) without the true owner's knowledge or consent, as with the Alicia McAteer case.

Identity fraud is creating a fictitious identity. Identity documents may be forged or legitimate documents fraudulently obtained. Identity fraud also happens when someone alters their own identity by making changes to name, date of birth, address, etc. for unlawful purposes.

With today's technology, the criminal mind can manufacture false identification quite easily. Stolen birth certificates, passports, driver's licenses, and social insurance cards are sold on the black market. "Novelty" pieces of identification are sold on the Internet and all it takes is one good piece of photo ID, along with your identity, for your house to be stolen out from under you. Just think back to your teenage years. How difficult was it to get a fake ID to get into a bar?

Who Says We Have a Problem?

Identity theft is the fastest growing crime in the world. It is the crime of the twenty-first century—the information age. Identity crimes are at the beginning of a whole range of major crimes, including people smuggling, drug trafficking, terrorism, money laundering, investment fraud, and mortgage and title fraud.

The more frequent crimes, which this book will examine more closely, involve fraud for illegal financial gains: the use of your good name for someone else's profit at your expense. Credit card fraud is estimated to cost the victim approximately $1,200 and can take over eighteen months to get the problems rectified.

Real-estate industry insiders now peg the average case of real estate fraud at $300,000, which means years of stress stemming from personal and financial repercussions for those who fall victim. According to the Quebec Association of Real Estate Agents and Brokers, mortgage fraud amounts to an estimated $1.5 billion per year, and even though other cities like Vancouver, Toronto, and Edmonton are hotbeds for this criminal activity, all Canadian homeowners are at risk. In 2000, real-estate title fraud claims accounted for only 6% of total claims at Canada's leading title insurance provider. Fast-forward five years, in 2005, and that number reached 33%.[1]

PhoneBusters, a national anti-fraud call centre, received calls from approximately 12,000 identity theft victims in 2005 and estimated losses at $8.7 million. In 2006, some 7,800 identity theft victims reported losses of $16.2 million. PhoneBusters estimates these numbers represent only a very small percentage of the actual losses as many victims do not report their incidents to this organization.[2]

The Interac Association reports that debit card fraud is increasing: in 2003, $44 million; in 2004, $60 million; and in 2005, $70.4 million. According to Detective Sgt. Dave Lollar of the OPP anti-rackets squad, this number may be much higher, as financial institutions do not disclose this information. The average debit card fraud amounts to $3000. In 2006, credit card thefts amounted to $291 million, bank robberies $5 million, and counterfeit currency $6 million.[3]

According to the findings of a 2003 Ipsos Reid survey, 9% of Canadians—or 2.7 million people—have fallen victim to identity theft at some point in their lives. These numbers probably include you or someone you know.

In the U.S., the FBI estimates that identity theft costs American businesses and consumers $50 billion per year and affects some 10 million victims annually. Fraud is estimated to account for 3 to 10% of the U.S. $2 trillion health care spending tab according to *USA Today*.

The proof is in. We are all at risk of becoming the next victim.

When Is It a Crime?

Possession of other person's identification is not a crime in Canada. Only when the identification is used to obtain credit, goods, services, or medical care in the name of another person can charges be laid under the Criminal Code. In the U.S., identity theft itself is a crime.

Why Steal an Identity?

A criminal steals someone's identity because 1) they are greedy or needy, 2) they have an opportunity to do so, 3) it is easy money, 4) the expectation of getting caught is fairly low, and 5) the punishment, if caught, is not very harsh.

Fraudsters who hide their identity by using someone else's include illegal immigrants wishing to stay in a country, people laundering money, drivers who have lost their driver's license, or possibly someone claiming to have certain educational qualifications to get a job.

Fraudsters may alter employment letters and T4 slips in order to qualify for credit cards, loans, or mortgages. This exaggerated income or possibly undeclared debts may do the trick in obtaining money or gaining access to credit.

Unsuspecting new immigrants to the country may fall prey to unlawful money brokers. The broker assists the immigrants in establishing their Canadian credit and applying for their first loan and credit card. A cash advance against the credit card for the limit is used to pay the broker.

A victim's health card might be used to gain access to health care professionals. The fraudster could be the patient or the doctor. In some cases, a routine check-up where all is well may result in a fabricated illness reported and billed for treatments that were never performed. Cosmetic treatments may be falsely reported for coverage, like claiming a nose restoration was necessary because of injuries from a non-existent car accident.

Criminals can generate millions of dollars every year by falsely advertising approved credit for non-qualifying borrowers provided they pay a fee in advance. The people who can least afford it, usually those with poor credit ratings, are often the key targets, and once the "loan processors" receive the money, they usually disappear.

Identity fraud and identity theft are crimes that exploit the weaknesses in our system. With collusion from an industry insider, these crimes can be very difficult to detect.

The Signs, Crimes, and Victims

What are some of the signs your identity may have been stolen?

- Your bills and account statements don't arrive when they are supposed to or not at all.
- Collection agencies or creditors call about accounts you don't have or bills that you have already paid.
- A credit-granting institution informs you that you have been approved or denied credit you have not applied for.
- Your banking statements show withdrawals or other transactions you didn't make.

- Your credit card statements show purchases or cash advances you didn't make.
- You are denied credit even though you believe you have a good credit record.
- You receive a Notice of Reassessment from the Canada Revenue Agency concerning your "undeclared" earnings.
- Your credit report shows debts that are not yours.

In credit crimes, you are guilty until you can prove you are innocent! It may be months, even years, before you realize someone is using your good name for his or her personal gain. Don't ignore the warning signals.

What Do Criminals Do with the Information?

The fraudulent, forged, or stolen identification such as your driver's license, social insurance card, birth certificate, citizenship card, passport, health card, military or employee ID card are used to apply for: credit cards, loans, mortgages, cell phones, purchases, medical service, other services, and maybe even be used to sell your home.

Computer-hacked credit card numbers are sold on the Internet. Within minutes of the sale of the information, that same credit card number may be used on several continents.

Seniors

According to PhoneBusters, seniors are targeted for many different reasons that include loneliness, lack of family support, age, vulnerability, and health-related reasons such as Alzheimer's. For a complete list of reasons and preventative measures for seniors please refer to Chapter 8: Fraud against Seniors.

Seniors are particularly susceptible to telephone fraud because their generation tends to be more trusting and less likely to hang up the telephone on someone who appears to be very friendly. The effects of this atrocious crime have re-

sulted in ruined families, great financial losses and even sui-
cide. Furthermore, seniors are more likely to have significant
savings and plenty of equity in their homes, which are likely
to be paid off; all available for the fraudsters to tap into.

Sometimes We Shoot Ourselves in the Foot

Over 100 victims had their personal information used so
criminals could apply for credit cards, driver's licenses, and
social insurance cards. The criminals racked up over
$500,000 worth in charges on fake credit cards before being
caught.

The victims had sent in their resumes in response to an
online employment ad. The candidates then received a letter
back promising a high-paying position. All they had to do
was send a $20 administration fee and complete the enclosed
form. The form requested information such as Social Insurance Number, driver's license number, full legal name, and
address.

The scam was discovered when a man complained to
Canada Post that he was no longer receiving his mail. Officials found his mail had been transferred though he'd never
requested it. Police tracked down the re-routed mail. They
have arrested two individuals and charged them with con-
spiracy to commit fraud.

The Twenty-Year-Old Student Loan

A collection agency calls a forty-five-year-old for a delin-
quent student loan. He has been out of school for over twenty
years and didn't borrow to fund his education. Is this a case
of stolen identity?

Lost Pay Cheque

A twenty-one-year-old woman was just paid last night.
The next morning, she makes a purchase with her debit card
at a convenience store only to discover she has no money left

in her account and now won't be able to pay her rent this week! Is this a case of stolen identity? How did they get her information? She has not lost her purse or ID.

Doctors Are Too Busy

A psychiatrist appeared to be seeing up to sixty-three patients a day. An investigation found that a former patient had stolen the doctor's billing identity, set up a counselling service, and billed Blue Cross for more than $1 million in services.

Easy Access to Personal Information

A teacher stole colleagues' pay stubs from campus mailboxes. The pay stubs along with a class list provided enough information for this fellow teacher to apply for fraudulent credit card accounts and steal $43,000 in merchandise using their names.

Doctors Make House Calls?

According to California's Blue Cross, more than 22,000 bills in 1990, ranging from $125 to $2,300, were issued from clinics working out of vans or temporary offices. These "clinics" use salespeople to recruit patients, but only those with health insurance. Free "preventive care" is offered and then the fraudsters claim for undetected illnesses and diagnostic tests never performed on the patient.

Overbilling

Medicare investigators found a group of diagnostic testing companies that used improperly obtained Medicare patient identification numbers to bill for the exams, which were likely never performed.

Short-Term Rental Is Now a Sale

An actress sublets her condo in Toronto so she can take

on a role in the U.S. only to return to find out her tenant sold her condo in the mere six months she was away.

Jobs Are Hard to Come By

As reported in *The Sentinel Reporter*, March 30, 2007, former Marine Charles Williams, Jr. was turned down four times for jobs. He said his job interviews seemed to go well, but after the criminal history check, he was turned down.

Williams paid an Internet background check company for a criminal report. When the results didn't match his history, he thought the company had given him the wrong report and thought nothing of it.

Williams applied for a part-time temporary job with JFC Insurance. Once again, he was turned down as a result of his criminal check. This time, the interviewer called him on his long list of felonies, which included drug charges, possession of cocaine, and domestic assault.

It finally sunk in; Williams had fallen victim to identity theft. About a year ago, he received a letter from Veterans Affairs. The letter informed him that his name was among veterans whose personal information was on a laptop stolen from the department. The letter also warned him that there was potential his identity would be stolen. Still, Williams was sure it wouldn't happen to him. That was his first mistake.

How Do They Get My Information?

Canadians are often too trusting and polite. When asked for information such as our birthday or our mother's maiden name, we will often respond without thinking, "Do they really need this information about me? How will this information be used?"

Mail Theft

Imagine one day you start getting calls from credit card companies for accounts you do not have. Your neighbour tells you she has noticed a new mailman. You watch closely as your mail is delivered. Shortly thereafter, another person comes to remove it and places mail in your mailbox. The next day, the same thing occurs. The mailman brings your mail and someone follows, removing it and putting other mail back in. You check the mail and it is your own. What is going on here?

Mail theft is one way your personal information is stolen. Fraudsters take your mail, open it to get your personal information, seal it back up and deliver it a day later. The fraudsters get the information they require through the access they have to your mail. Your cancelled cheques provide your signature when returned with your bank statement. Fraudsters remove the credit card bills, which are truly not yours. In a matter of weeks, they are gone, and you are now left literally holding the bills.

Phony Ads

Some companies claim they guarantee you a loan even if you have a bad credit history or no credit rating at all. They may request an upfront fee of several hundred dollars. If you send your money to these companies, it is unlikely you will get your promised loan or your prepaid fee back.

Inside Job

Disgruntled or easily persuaded employees may divulge large amounts of personal information for a price, breaching the confidentiality of their company or organization.

Authorization for a credit check is often given to a landlord as they assess your eligibility to become a renter in their property. Your personal information may be used dishonestly in fraudulent matters when it was given in good faith.

Dumpster Diving

Crooks go through your trash and recycling to collect valuable information about you. Materials of particular interest include discarded credit card applications, bank statements, credit card statements, receipts, and any documents that contain your personal information.

Shoulder Surfing

Crooks may eavesdrop on your public conversations to obtain personal data or watch you type in your personal identification number (PIN) at a bank machine.

Computer Hacking

Crooks steal personal information from computer databases by using spyware. This could be from your personal computer or the target could be a corporate giant. The information may be used directly or sold for a third party to use.

Phishing and Spoofing

Crooks send an e-mail impersonating a trusted company asking you to respond with personal information.

Spam

Crooks send an e-mail requiring you to respond to alleged contests. In one case, thieves sent out e-mails promising tickets to *The Oprah Winfrey Show* to those who replied with their personal information.

Wireless Communication

Unsecured wireless transmissions may be intercepted from cordless phones, wireless computers, and cell phones.

In Chapter 4, we have extensive coverage on Internet and E-mail Fraud. From spam to spoofing, from pharming to phishing, we cover many of the schemes that fraudsters are using to steal your personal information and your assets. You will also find a complete list of things you can do to protect you and your computer.

Document Theft

Your purse or wallet may be stolen and there go your identitification documents. Your home, office, or car could be broken into. In today's market, the information taken is even more valuable than your TV or stereo.

How Can I Protect Myself?

Before it happens to you, you have two options. Your first option is to do nothing. Your second option is to start taking control of your situation and minimize the risk of becoming the next victim.

Let's face it, you cannot absolutely prevent having your identity stolen. Criminals can commit identity theft relatively easily because of lax credit industry practices, the careless handling of information in our workplaces, and the ease of obtaining personal information. And sometimes we are the ones who give away our information innocently. If someone really wants to steal your identity, they will.

You can reduce your risk of becoming the next victim by following these tips:

Destroying Confidential Documents and Records
Strip shred it:

Strip shredders are generally less expensive than crosscut shredders. They cut the paper in long strands that the serious criminal can reassemble. Shredding high volumes of material and mixing non-confidential documents in with the confidential will reduce the risk of this happening.

Crosscut shred it:

The crosscut shredder offers a higher degree of security when you shred. There is no hope of reassembling a document that has been run through a crosscut shredder.

Burn it:

If you come up with a document that is particularly sensitive and you don't want to chance that it might be reassembled—no matter how slim that chance might be—toss it in the fire and ensure it is burned in its entirety.

Recycle it:

Only recycle non-personal paper items. Remove your name and address label from magazines. Do not put dated birthday cards or instant-approval credit card applications in your blue box.

Guarding Your Personal Information

Identification documents:

Remove your birth certificate and social insurance card from your wallet or purse. Keep them in a safety deposit box or somewhere very secure. Carry only the cards and identification you really need. Carry your passport only when travelling, and when not travelling, keep it in a secure place.

Secure your important papers:

Rent a safety deposit box to store key identification documents as well as important papers such as tax returns, diplomas and degrees, marriage certificate, wills, power of attorney, and insurance policies. Shred or burn any unnecessary documents containing personal information.

- Do not leave sensitive financial information accessible to family members, domestic employees, friends, or neighbours.
- Be stingy in giving out your personal information.
- Know whom you are giving your information to. Never share personal information unless you initiated the contact and the information is absolutely necessary.

• Do not give out personal information to unsolicited e-mails or phone calls.

• Avoid cordless phones, cell phones, and wireless Internet routers when giving out personal information. Signals can be intercepted.

Mail:

Lock your mailbox, install a mail slot in your door, or have the mail delivered to the community, group, apartment, or business mailbox. Pick up your mail as soon as possible after it's been delivered.

When going on vacation, have a neighbour pick up your mail or place mail on hold with Canada Post. Allow three business days for Canada Post to get the "hold" in place. A small fee applies and this can be done online or in person.

If you receive a letter not belonging to you, write "not at this address" and deposit it in a red street letterbox or the outgoing mail slot of the community mailbox. Place your mail in a closed secure mailbox.

When mailing sensitive information (business or financial) or large quantities of mail, deposit it at your local post office or courier the important documents.

Computers and Internet:

When making a purchase online, be certain the Internet site is secure by checking for the lock or key symbol on the browser status bar and ensuring it is closed and not open. Avoid cordless phones, cell phones, and wireless Internet routers when giving out personal information. Signals can be intercepted. Don't use automatic login features that save your user name and password. See Chapter 4: Internet and E-Mail Fraud for more details on computer and Internet safety such as antivirus, anti-spyware, firewalls, etc.

Credit cards:

Insist your new credit card be sent to your local bank or credit union branch for pick-up rather than being mailed to your home. Routinely track your credit card activity and match it to your spending. Be sure your credit card statements arrive on time or switch to e-mail delivery. Cancel all your unused or unnecessary credit cards.

Handling Banking Records
Debit cards:

Never write down your personal identification number (PIN) and leave it in your wallet or other obvious place. Select a PIN that is difficult to guess, not your birthday or phone number.

Make sure no one can see you type in your PIN at an automated banking machine or at a point-of-sale terminal by covering the keypad with your hand.

Keep an eye on your banking card. Do not let it go out of your sight. This is how "skimming" occurs. Skimming is when your card is swiped in a machine that steals the personal information off the magnetic strip on the back of your card. The information is then put on a fraudulent card and the crooks go on a shopping spree or empty your bank account. They need your PIN to complete this scam and they usually get that by shoulder surfing or through a hidden camera. When conducting a transaction at the point-of-sale, only allow your card to be swiped once.

Do not share your account numbers, access codes, and PIN with anyone, not even family members.

Automated banking machines (ABMs):

Only use ABMs located in financial institutions and businesses you are familiar with. Be sure the face of the machine looks right before proceeding. Some of the latest technology has a green card insert over the card insertion space. This makes it difficult for fraudsters to overlay the machine with their own skimming technology as they attempt to steal your debit card number and PIN.

In the instance you become a victim of debit card fraud, the Canadian Code of Practice for Consumer Debit Card Services protects you, under which all proven victims of debit card fraud will not suffer any financial losses.

Be alert as you go into an ABM vestibule, especially at night. Robberies, though rare, could happen. Should you fall victim, for your own safety, comply with the robber's demands.

For more details on credit and debit cards, please see Chapter 2: Debit and Credit Card Fraud.

Bill payments:

Pay your bills via an automatic account debit or by telephone banking rather than by mailing a paper cheque.

Telephone banking:

Use a hard phone line, not a cordless phone, when doing telephone banking because signals can be intercepted. Monitor your bank and credit card accounts frequently, daily if possible.

Cheques and bank statements:

When a cheque is required, sign it with a fine-point permanent marker that cannot be erased. Decline the return cheque option with your bank statement to prevent a mail thief from having your signature too. Better yet, opt for an electronic statement so no paper will hit your mailbox.

Financial check up:

Review your credit reports annually, or more often if you want. Be sure to check every line of information on the credit bureau report. When sensitive information is being shared with your bank or credit union account manager, be sure your conversation cannot be overheard.

Credit monitoring services:

Several companies, including the three credit bureaus, offer credit-monitoring services for an annual fee ranging from $50 to $120 per year. They notify you when there is any activity on your credit report, thus alerting you to possible fraud and limiting the possible loss and damage to your credit rating. If you decide to subscribe, be sure to choose a service that monitors all three credit reports on an ongoing basis. One drawback is that the notification comes after the fact that someone has tapped into your identity and has applied for credit, but the sooner you know, the better!

Obtaining Identity Theft Coverage

There are numerous identity theft insurance products available to consumers. Be sure to read and understand what coverage is being offered and compare the values.

Though we are often not held to repay fraudulent credit card purchases or money fraudulently taken from our bank or credit union accounts, identity theft coverage may reimburse you for expenses you incur as you clean up your credit history such as legal fees and other expenses.

If you wish to purchase identity theft coverage, consider those available as a free or low-cost rider on an existing insurance policy. Some one-time fee options are available along with your title insurance policy or, in rare cases, may be included with your property or fire insurance policy. Be sure to understand what you are getting from whom, for how long, and for how much. Please see Chapter 3: Credit Reports for complete details.

Do I have to Give Out My Social Insurance Number (SIN)?

The SIN was created in 1964 to serve as a client account number in the administration of the Canada Pension Plan and Canada's employment insurance programs. In 1967, what is now Canada Revenue Agency (CRA) started using the SIN for tax reporting purposes.

Organizations inside and outside of government ask for the SIN because it is a simple and unique method of identification. Many use it as a client account number to save them from setting up their own numbering systems. Although only certain government departments are authorized to collect and use the SIN, there is no legislation that stops other organizations from asking for it.

Your Social Insurance Number record is protected under the Privacy Act and no individual or company, other than authorized government agencies, can access information from that record. Credit bureaus are not government agencies and cannot access your Social Insurance Number record.

If another person uses your SIN for employment purposes or to receive other taxable income, you will receive a Notice of Reassessment from the Canada Revenue Agency concerning the undeclared earnings. This is an indication that your SIN is being used fraudulently. Report this immediately to the nearest office of Service Canada Centre.

The 900-series Social Insurance Numbers must now have an expiry date on them. On April 3, 2004, all 900-series cards expired and new ones were issued with an expiry date. These cards are not issued to people who are Canadian citizens or permanent residents but instead to those who need a SIN for employment purposes or to comply with other authorized uses. Holders of 900-series SINs include temporary foreign workers and refugee claimants. The expiry dates coincide with the end of the SIN holder's authorization to stay in Canada.

I Am a Victim of Identity Theft—What Can I Do?
* Act immediately!
* File a police report.
* Place a fraud alert on all three of your credit bureau reports to prevent unauthorized credit from being issued. (See the appendix Credit Reporting Agencies for contact information.)
* Notify all the banks, credit unions, and credit card companies where you have financial accounts and request an alert be placed on your accounts.
* Notify the respective institutions, Ministry of Transportation, Service Canada, Health Card issuer, etc.

Identity Theft Statement
An Identity Theft Statement is a great tool to use if you become a victim. This may be used to report and record the details of your incident to financial institutions, credit card companies and other companies, where fraudulent activities have occurred against you. The statement will tell them that you did not create the debt or charges and give them the information they need to start an investigation. By completing the statement, you are not guaranteed that the identity thief will be prosecuted or that the debt or charges will be cleared, but this process may stop this from happening again and you may get exonerated of all charges and debts incurred due to the thief's actions. Those who endorse this Identity Theft Statement include all of Canada's major banks, Sears, HBC, Canadian Tire, and some other large financial institutions and credit card companies.

Once you complete the statement, keep a copy of all originals and correspondence for every statement you send out. Don't send originals of any documents; only copies. Also, keep track of the details of your calls and correspondence, taking note of whom you spoke to and when. For complete instructions on how to complete the Identity Theft Statement and a copy of the actual form, please see the appendix. You can also get an online form at: http://www.phonebusters.com/images/IDTheftStatement.pdf

Lost Passports

Report the loss or theft of your passport immediately to Passport Canada by calling 1-800-567-6868. If outside Canada, report it to the nearest Canadian Government office, embassy, consulate, or in person at a Passport Office. By mail: Passport Canada, Foreign Affairs and International Trade Canada, Gatineau, Quebec, K1A 0G3

Lost SIN Card

If your SIN card has been lost or stolen, it is important to be aware that someone could try to use your Social Insurance Number. Report the loss or theft of your card to the police. Ask for the case reference number, and the officer's name and telephone number. Next, contact Service Canada at 1-800-206-7218 and select "information on Social Insurance Numbers" from the voice menu. By mail: Service Canada, Social Insurance Registration Office, P.O. Box 7000, Bathurst, New Brunswick, E2A 4T1

Credit Bureau Agencies

See appendix for complete details on all three Canadian credit reporting agencies.

Support Agencies
PhoneBusters:

The Canadian Anti-Fraud Call Centre is a national service operated by law enforcement agencies that collects information about identity theft, records complaints, forwards information to the appropriate law enforcement agencies, and offers advice to victims. The PhoneBusters organization endorses the Identity Theft Statement and you can access the form on their website.

Toll free phone: 1-888-495-8501
Website: www.phonebusters.com
E-mail: info@phonebusters.com

The Office of the Privacy Commissioner of Canada:

The Office of the Privacy Commissioner can investigate data breaches that may lead to personal information being used to commit identity theft. They can identify weaknesses in the systems of a private-sector organization or government department and help it to close gaps and prevent further data breaches.

Some provinces have adopted their own private-sector privacy laws, which are enforced by provincial privacy commissioners:

Quebec: http://www.cai.gouv.qc.ca
Alberta: http://www.oipc.ab.ca
British Columbia: http://www.oipc.bc.ca
General Inquiries: Toll-free: 1-800-282-1376
Phone: (613) 995-8210

Reporting Economic Crime Online (RECOL):

RECOL is an initiative that involves an integrated partnership between international, federal, and provincial law enforcement agencies as well as with regulators and private commercial organizations that have a legitimate investigative interest in receiving a copy of complaints of economic crimes. RECOL will recommend the appropriate law enforcement or regulatory agency and/or private commercial organization for potential investigation.

Personal Information Protection and Electronic Documents Act (PIPEDA):

Since January 1, 2001, PIPEDA applied to personal information about customers or employees that is collected, used, or disclosed by the federally regulated sector in the course of commercial activities. It also applies to information that is sold across provincial and territorial boundaries. As of January 1, 2004, the act covers the collection, use, and disclosure of personal information in the course of any commercial activity within a province, including provincially regulated organizations, except in provinces that have enacted legislation that is deemed to be substantially similar to the federal law.

Under the new law, organizations such as banks, telecommunications companies, and airlines cannot require you to consent to the collection, use, or disclosure of your personal information unless it is required for a specific and legitimate purpose. An organization may disclose information for several reasons: in order to comply with a court order, if they suspect the information relates to matters of national security of because of an emergency that threatens the life, health, or security of an individual.

This means that unless an organization can demonstrate that law requires your SIN, or that no alternative identifier would suffice to complete the transaction, you cannot be denied a product or service on the grounds of your refusal to provide your SIN.

In Canada, when computer systems are hacked into or information lost or stolen from companies we do business with, Canadian laws do not force these companies to disclose the breach in privacy. The public does not usually hear of the cases where our information may have been breached.

In January 2007, consumers were shaken by the news that millions of credit card accounts may have been compromised after hackers stole customer information from computer systems TJX Cos., the U.S. parent firm of Canadian retailers Winners and HomeSense. This disclosure came as a result of U.S. laws, which require the publication of this information.

Each year, tens of thousands of people fall victim to identity theft. It takes time to report to your financial service providers and other service providers the fact that your personal information has been compromised. Identity theft wreaks havoc on your ability to borrow and to function in your daily life. Fraud alerts on your credit bureaus will cause headaches for years to come as you get scrutinized as though you were the criminal when in fact it was you that placed the alert so as to stop further damage to yourself and others from suffering financial losses. Annoying calls from collection agencies and late-payment notices in the mail may cause you frustration and anger. You may lose hours at work and suffer emotional and mental distress as you try to prove your innocence.

Insurance companies are trying to educate us. Fraud drives up the cost of health care, which in turn forces employers to raise our premiums and lower our benefits. You may be denied a job after a potential employer checks into your history. The privilege of renting an apartment or of buying a home is at risk. You may be denied a much-needed loan or mortgage. You may be denied your right to drive, as you may not be allowed to renew your driver's license. In extreme cases, you may even be wrongly accused of criminal activity and falsely arrested.

In the end, we all pay the price. It comes in the form of higher service fees and higher interest rates. Identity thieves and fraudsters are seldom arrested and charged. It's an easy crime to perpetrate and will be repeated again and again.

Chapter 2

Debit and Credit Card Fraud

Just imagine: You are rushing about to get ready for your family vacation to the East Coast. You are finalizing all the little details as your spouse and the kids pack the car for your big drive across Canada. You call to cancel the newspaper and you have left the mail key with the next-door neighbour, who will empty your community mailbox and keep an eye on the house while you are gone. You've got the drapes pulled, the plants watered, a picnic lunch packed, and have set the lights on timers throughout the house. And in the car we go—at last, you can relax!

Your husband has promised a quick stop at the local department store for a new game for the Nintendo DS to occupy the kids on the long drive. It's a great idea and a good investment along with a few special treats and comic books. At the checkout your spouse runs his debit card through the machine. Oops, it didn't take. The clerk says, "Here let me try." She drops the card on the floor out of your eyesight. She runs the card through the debit card machine for you and watches as you push in your secret personal identification number. It worked that time, and off to the races you go. Isn't this day and age of technology wonderful?

After a long day of driving and only a quick bathroom break, you make it to your first overnight stop. You check in, drop your bags in the room, and head off to a local diner. After dinner, you go to pay for the meal with your debit card. Oops, yet again, it's not working on the first try. "That happened earlier today," you explain to the waitress. "Run it through again." This time, the clerk explains, "The card has come back declined, do you have another form of payment to cover your bill?" You're embarrassed as others are waiting in line behind you to pay. You are perplexed, then angry, and then provide her with your credit card. Thank goodness that worked.

When you get back to your hotel room, you call your bank only to discover your trip savings have been cleared out of your account and the balance is almost zero. What a terrible start to your family vacation!

Debit Cards

We all enjoy the convenience that the automatic banking machine (ABM) and debit card provide us 24-hours a day. Regrettably, so do criminals. According to many industry experts and the Better Business Bureau, bank fraud is one of the fastest growing crimes in North America. When you insert your card into an ABM, what you may not know is that at the same time, criminals may also be collecting your personal information to access your account.

Debit card fraud is a crime that banks take very seriously. According to the Canadian Bankers Association, in 2005, only a fraction of 1% (0.2%) of debit cards was used fraudulently. The key to your accounts is your personal identification number (PIN). When a cardholder enters their PIN into the card reader, it is scrambled using state-of-the-art encryption technology before it is sent through the network to the cardholder's financial institution. The PIN is not contained on the debit card's magnetic strip and only the card owner should therefore know the PIN.

The financial institutions comprehend that being the victim of debit card fraud can be upsetting for a customer. The Canadian Bankers Association states on their website that "if this does happen, banks will immediately look into the matter and get the money back to the customer as quickly as possible, which usually happens within a week."[4] During this stressful time, financial institutions work with customers to deal with any financial commitments.

The banks frequently look for ways to enhance the protection of their customers. Canadian financial institutions are moving to chip cards. This small microcomputer contains the information on the card needed to process transactions. The chip is extremely difficult to duplicate, so this is an added level of security. It will be similar to a debit card with respect to the PIN. Industry officials from the credit card industry have stated recently that by the year 2010, most credit cards will be replaced with this new chip technology. As cards reach expiry, they will be replaced with cards containing the new chips. Eventually, all retail outlets will have new devices that will be able to read the chips.

Until this new technology is widely available, there will always be a threat of someone trying to gain control of your debit and credit cards for illegitimate purposes. Although there is no guarantee that this new security feature will completely eliminate credit and debit card fraud, it will act as a great deterrent since it will take longer and cost more to crack. This may not be economically feasible for most thieves.

There are many ways for thieves to obtain your debit card number and PIN, including skimming, shoulder surfing, phishing, pharming, pin-hole-sized cameras, and keypad overlays. Debit card theft occurs at bank machines, in retail outlets, and throughout the Internet.

Skimmers are electronic devices used on some ABMs to steal card details such as name, address, telephone number, card number, and credit limit. Information obtained with these skimming devices can be uploaded to the Internet in minutes and used to make counterfeit cards in a matter of hours. Skimming can also take place at a retail outlet such as a restaurant or gas station, where an unscrupulous employee brings in their own card reader. They will read the card for the legitimate transaction once and scan the card a second time in their own card reader, skimming the information to recreate your card.

The next step is getting your PIN, which they have conveniently obtained through a hidden camera above you while you entered your PIN or a through a pressure sensitive keypad overlay. With the card information from the skimmer and the PIN number from the camera, they can begin depleting your bank account up to its daily limit within hours. You should always question why a retail establishment runs your card more than once and look for any other suspicious behaviour. Always ask for the voided slip from the retailer.

Shoulder surfing is quite easy since all someone has to do is look over your shoulder and watch you key in your PIN. Once they have the PIN, they now need your card. The thieves are quite creative when it comes to getting the card, so protect it like cash and always be cautious when keying in your PIN in a card reader. If someone is too close to you, either ask them to back away or don't complete the transaction. Get into the habit of shielding your PIN entry with your other hand. If there are people loitering near the ABM, it is probably wise not to use that machine.

Phishing is a scam where customers are duped into entering personal information such as PIN number, credit card number, Social Insurance Number, or account number via a bogus e-mail or website form. The e-mail or website usually looks authentic as though it were sent by a real company.

They are, however, simply fronts for a scam. The messages contained within the e-mail usually have some sense of urgency to trigger an impulsive reaction by the victim. They may even go as far as telling you that you are a victim of identity fraud. Once they get your personal information, they will use it to create fraudulent cards and then gain access to your bank accounts, credit cards, or even create your identity and do other major crimes such as stealing the title to your home.

The best way to outsmart the criminal during a phishing expedition is to not select any links and by immediately deleting the e-mail. Remember, reputable companies will never ask you to give your personal information via an e-mail or on a website when you are already a client of that company. In some phishing instances, criminals request that the recipients download and install "security" software attached to the spam e-mail. If a recipient installs the software, the criminals can monitor the victim's computer and capture the details of bank accounts and debit cards. The use of this mechanism, though low in relation to other mechanisms, has recently showed an increasing trend.

If you are not sure of the request being made, contact the company using an officially published phone number or use the number on the back of your card or on your bank/credit card statement.

Pharming (also known as DNS poisoning) is very similar to phishing but it doesn't include the e-mail as bait. The criminals try to steal personal information from many people simultaneously through domain spoofing. The hackers take over a DNS server and try to redirect user information to a new site that they use to illegally gather personal information such as your debit card information, including your PIN. If the pharming site is a copy of your bank's site, they can use this to gain enormous amounts of information, and most users wouldn't know they were on the bogus site because it is so well produced to look like the legitimate site. The more sophisticated the hackers get, the easier it is for them to set up these pharming sites. Another version of pharming is keystroke logging which is discussed in greater detail in Chapter 4: Internet and E-Mail Fraud.

We recently attended a seminar where the local police hosted a session on identity theft and fraud. They showcased a camera and a keypad overlay. The criminals had set up a camera in a brochure rack beside the keypad and they had placed their own card reader skimmer over the official ABM reader. The activity was stopped when the fraudulent card reader became loose and someone contacted the bank that owned the ABM. This type of debit card fraud is extremely rewarding for the thieves because they can net a few hundred cards with matching PINs in one night and retrieve the camera and fake card reader after all the information is extracted. If you suspect your ABM has any loose equipment or looks as if it was tampered with, contact your financial institution and don't use that ABM.

A famous trick used by some scam artists to obtain your debit card and PIN is called the Lebanese Loop. This is where a plastic envelope is made up to fit in the card slot perfectly so you can't see it. The machine knows your card is inserted but can't read it. Usually, a "good samaritan" sees this happening and explains that the same thing happened to them last week. They then tell you to try the PIN input a few times while they watch you. When this fails, they advise you to go to your bank the next day to get your card back. Once you leave, they pull out the plastic envelope with your card and off they go with your money after they shoulder surfed and got your PIN while you were struggling with the card stuck in the machine. If the ABM takes your card while you are trying to do a transaction, it is really important that you don't let anyone see you input you PIN. You should be very cautious of strangers trying to assist you at the ABM.

Avoiding ABM Fraud

Choosing an ABM

- Pick your ABM carefully and always remember your personal safety is very important.
- Make a habit of using the same ABM as much as possible, and if you notice something out of the ordinary, contact your financial institution or the owner of the machine.
- ABMs inside a business and during business hours with security cameras are less likely to be targeted by criminals.

Using the ABM

- Watch out for shoulder surfers or people who stand too close to you; be alert.
- Check the card reader out to ensure there are no overlays or plastic inserts.
- Cancel your transaction if you feel uncomfortable.
- Never allow yourself to be distracted by strangers while doing your transaction.
- Shield your PIN entry with your hand or body.
- Don't accept help from "good samaritans" at the ABM.

Leaving the ABM

- Discreetly put your money and card away upon completion of your transaction.
- Take your paper transaction receipt home and dispose of it like any other sensitive personal document. Don't leave it in the trash can beside the ABM.
- If the ABM does not return your card, report this to your financial institution immediately.
- Check your bank activity regularly—even daily, if possi-

ble. The sooner you spot and report suspicious account activity, the better.

Using Your PIN

- Memorize your PIN.
- Do not allow anyone to use your card or PIN.
- Choose your PIN carefully. Avoid an obvious number such as a birthdate or phone number.
- Never write your PIN on your card or leave it in your purse or wallet.
- Always shield your PIN entry from anyone nearby.
- Never give your PIN to anyone, even if they say they are from your bank, Interac, law enforcement, or if they say they are investigating fraud from your financial institution.

In addition to all of the above, it is really important that you keep an eye on your debit card at all times even when it is being swiped at a retail outlet. You should always know where your card is at all times. Keep your card in a safe place and treat it like cash. If you suspect someone knows your PIN, change it immediately or contact your financial institution to cancel the card and get a new one. If you suspect you have been a victim of debit card fraud, contact you financial institution immediately. You also may want to follow up your phone call with a letter.

It is also good to take note that the Canadian Code of Practice for Consumer Debit Card Services protects consumers in Canada, and all proven victims of debit card fraud will not suffer any financial losses. This code was developed through consultation with many groups in the retail and banking industries as well as various government agencies and consumer groups.

Credit Cards

There was a recent case where a woman was dining at her favourite restaurant at which she had been a patron for over ten years. She noticed her server was new to the restaurant and welcomed her. The waitress was very friendly. She left the server a nice tip since she did a professional job throughout the meal. She paid by credit card, as she always did in the past, thinking nothing of it as this new employee walked away with it. A few weeks later, she was shocked when she received her next credit card bill. She saw all kinds of charges amounting to several thousands of dollars for things that she didn't buy.

Credit card fraud is increasing to the point where it costs businesses across North America billions of dollars each year. Businesses are forced to pass these costs on to consumers in the form of higher prices. Victims of credit card scams suffer in many ways, such as time lost at work and the time required to get their credit cleared. The entire process is very inconvenient. If you are a victim of credit card fraud, you are not usually required to pay for any unauthorized charges. You should contact your credit card company as soon as possible to reduce your liability.

When the restaurant victim called her credit card company, they said she was a target of "skimming," a growing area of credit card theft similar to the debit card technique described previously. At the restaurant, an employee probably ran her credit card twice: once for the meal charge and a second time on a magnetic card reader. The employee then copied the data onto a blank credit card and sold it to a third person or used it personally. The victim didn't have to pay for the unauthorized charges.[5]

In today's society, it is quite common to make routine purchases with a credit card since it is so convenient. It is easy to prevent credit card theft, and financial institutions are trying to assist consumers by offering various methods of pre-

vention. Some of these preventative measures include: pho-
tographs of the cardholder on the card, holograms, hidden
images, and secret imprints. All of these make it difficult for
thieves to recreate a card with a stolen credit card number.
Treat your credit card like cash, just as you should with your
debit card. In 2006, credit card theft topped $291 million,
compared to $5 million stolen in bank robberies and $6 million in counterfeit money.[6] Not all credit card theft is reported
by everyone concerned, so this number could be higher.
Credit card companies and financial institutions are not required by law to report all of their credit card thefts.

Credit Card fraud is an international black-market affair
with organized crime and other groups using the Internet to
buy and sell credit card information on a regular basis. The
evolution of this major crime has grown with the popularity
of the Internet and the growth of technology worldwide. Recently, a popular American network television show set up a
sting operation with fake stolen cards, a fake website with
popular items bought by the thieves, and a fake delivery service to deliver the goods. Within hours of selling the cards on
the underground black market through the Internet, they were
in use and purchases were made off the website with the
"stolen cards." The merchandise was then delivered and
tracked to innocent individuals who had been duped into online romances with the card thieves living in other countries.

One of the unsuspecting Americans who had been duped
was even using his own money to reroute the goods to Africa
and Europe. Eventually, the TV producers had the duped
American work with them to lead them to one of the players
on the other side of the Atlantic. There were no arrests made,
but the entire scope of this illegal trade in stolen credit cards
was unraveled right in front of millions of TV viewers. It bog-
gles the mind to think how bold and aggressive these thieves
are as they go about their routine. The cost to all concerned
is enormous. The online love affair was all a setup to get the

American to assist the credit card thieves with the receipt of their purchased goods. Once they won their hearts, they were able to get them to assist in procuring the receipt and delivery of the goods. They had no idea what was going on behind the scenes.

Although you may not be held accountable for fraudulent purchases made on your credit card, someone is out the merchandise, and now the money, as these bills get charged back and you are refunded. In the end, we all pay the price.

Retailers today blank out the majority of your credit card number on your receipt to protect you should the receipt fall into unscrupulous hands. (Be aware, this may not be the practice in all areas.)

Protect Your Credit Card

Common sense is the best rule of thumb when it comes to your credit card. You should never lend your card to anyone else. If you want someone else to use your credit card, go with the person and do it yourself. Some other tips include[7]:

- Only carry one or, at most, two credit cards.
- Don't write your PIN on your credit card. This prevents thieves from using your card and PIN to withdraw money at an ABM machine.
- Write down the phone numbers of the credit card companies and keep them in a safe place to have them handy if a credit card is lost or stolen.
- Immediately report lost or stolen cards to the credit card company. The credit card company can stop the thief by cancelling your credit card and number.

Guard Your Credit Card Number

Your credit card number is an extremely important piece of information as it is the main part of a credit card transaction. More frequently than not, thieves are creating new cards with the number alone and they don't need your card to perform this illegal procedure. They can also use your number to make purchases over the telephone or through e-mail.

It is not unusual to receive credit card offers in the mail. If you don't intend on using these credit cards, we suggest you destroy the documents using a paper shredder. Also, consider the following:

- Watch out for people shoulder surfing (someone looking over your shoulder) when you are checking out at a store.
- Be cautious with your credit card number and security PIN. Make sure you know to whom you are giving your credit card number when dealing with telemarketers and Internet purchases. There are many con artists who pretend to be legitimate companies on the telephone and on the Internet.
- Verify all of your credit card transactions. Some dishonest retailers may change your credit card slip after you sign it.
- Never leave any blank spaces on your credit card slips where a scam artist can fill in additional amounts. You should always add up the total before signing.
- Credit card companies will never call you to ask for your card number or security PIN. Therefore, never provide this information to anyone on the telephone or on the Internet.
- No matter the circumstances, you should never sign a blank credit card slip.

Check Those Receipts

With respect to receipts from credit card purchases, it is important to collect them all and match them against your monthly statements. If you discard them, you should do so with care such as a cross-shredder or tear them into tiny pieces. You could even burn them in the fireplace if you wish.

Never put them out in your garbage or paper recycle because thieves check for these receipts as well as credit card statements in the garbage. The wealth of information on the receipt and statements is enough to start an identity theft process. Be sure to do the following at all times:

- Keep all your credit card receipts and verify them against your monthly paper statement or online statement for accuracy.
- Notify your credit card company of any unauthorized use.
- Destroy all of your recipts and statements with a shredder once you have verifeid their accuracy.

In order to reduce the chances of credit card fraud from happening to you, it is advisable to sign the back of your new cards as soon as you receive them and destroy any old cards you no longer need. Or you can try something different. We recently attended an event where a specialist in identity theft from the First Canadian Title insurance company told a story about local police officers who started a new trend in credit card protection: they started writing the following on the back of all their credit cards instead of signing the card: "Please ask for photo ID." We surveyed over twenty retail cashiers in the Greater Toronto Area and asked them what they would do if they saw that on the back of a credit card and they all said they would ask for a photo before completing the transaction. From this little impromptu survey, we feel comfortable telling you that this ounce of prevention can go far in stopping some of the fraud with credit cards. Until we all have electronic chips in our cards that can't be copied, we are all vulnerable to credit card fraud and identity theft.

After reviewing all of the various websites for all the major banks and credit card companies, as well as thorough research on credit cards, we have the following additional tips to prevent credit card fraud:

- Only use one of your credit cards to make online purchases. This is great for tracking purposes.
- Use only one card to purchase gas. This is another good way to keep track of your purchases and monitor any fraudulent activity.
- Cancel all unused credit cards. The fewer cards you own, the less damage you will suffer if you are a victim of identity theft or a lost or stolen wallet or purse.
- Get extra security such as PIN, password, or chip technology, if available.
- Never sign a blank credit card application. You open yourself to fraud if you sign any blank form.
- Never lend your credit card to anyone. They might not have the same security habits that you have or they may even abuse the card with unwanted purchases that end up on your account.
- Insist that your new credit card be mailed to your bank branch, not your home, if possible.
- Pay attention to the expiry dates on all your credit cards. If your replacement card doesn't arrive the month prior to the expiry date, notify the card issuer as someone may have stolen the card.
- Review your credit report annually and question any credit inquiries or unauthorized accounts immediately. (See Chapter 3: Credit Reports for more details.)

The same techniques for obtaining information that we mentioned earlier for debit cards applies to credit cards; these include skimming, phishing, pharming, shoulder surfing, and dumpster diving. You should never give any information about your credit card, such as numbers and security PINs, to anyone on the Internet whom you don't know. This also applies to incoming phone calls requesting the same information. Your financial institution would never e-mail or call you for these details.

Never leave your credit cards unattended at your workplace because this is a common area that thieves target. Guard your credit cards like cash. Would you leave cash unattended, free for someone to pick up? Another area of concern with credit cards is leaving them in a glove compartment of a car. Thieves know this and target cars for this easy loot. An alarmingly high proportion of credit card thefts occur in this manner.

Victim Action Plan

If you are a victim, you should be prepared to act quickly. It is recommended that you have a record of all your card numbers as well as the card issuer's phone number so you can call the appropriate number to report any fraudulent activity, theft, or lost cards. If you are a victim of credit card fraud, contact your credit card issuer immediately as well as the local police. Some people choose not to call the police, but calling them is the right thing to do if you want to stop this type of crime. The police may have similar cases in your area or where this crime took place. By sharing your story with them, you can assist in catching the criminals and stopping this type of criminal activity. Keep a copy of the police report should you require evidence in the future to prove your innocence.

You should also keep a record of whom you called as well as the details of the conversation and what action will take place after the call. An Identity Theft Statement form is available in the appendix if you need to complete a written report for the credit card issuer and police. This form is described in greater detail in the first chapter. You can also access this form on the PhoneBusters website and Industry Canada website. (Please see the website information in the appendix.)

Chapter 3

Credit Reports

An essential part of determining whether you have been a victim of identity theft is to regularly review your credit report at least once a year. You must know what to look for and what to do if anything needs correcting. In this chapter, we will explain what a credit report is, how to read a report, how to obtain a report, how to correct errors, and how to improve your score.

According to the American Federal Trade Commission, who regularly tracks identity theft activity in the United States, identity theft complaints are broken down as follows[8]:

- About 50% reported that a credit card was opened in their name.
- 25% reported that the thief established a telephone, cell phone, or another service in their name.
- 16% reported that a bank account was opened in their name or unauthorized withdrawals had been made from their account.
- 9% reported that the thief obtained a loan in their name.
- 8% reported that the thief obtained a fraudulent document such as a driver's license.

It is fair to say that Canada has a similar economy as the U.S. and similar fraud activities take place on both sides of the border. These statistics make it imperative that you monitor your own credit reports and understand what they mean to your financial well-being. The thieves are going after your identity to gain access to your money and other assets. If identity theft is stopped early enough, it can cause you less grief and save you lots of time and money in the long run.

What Is a Credit Report?

A credit report contains information about your financial behaviour and it shows how you have used your credit with respect to your debt obligations and how responsible you have acted. If you are late making credit card payments or behind in your loan installments, the credit report will have a record of this derogatory action. In Canada, credit reports are prepared by three credit reporting agencies (see appendix 3, Credit Reporting Agencies, for their contact details) based upon information provided voluntarily by financial institutions and other lenders. In addition to information from the lenders and institutions, the agencies also gather data from the courts and public records such as bankruptcies, foreclosures, and liens.

Your credit history is like your favourite sweatshirt: it will stay with you long after you first got it. It will show that coffee stain on the front and the pull on the side. Just as you would not subject your sweatshirt to hard bleaching, you must also take care of your credit history.

Maintaining a good credit record is very important since lenders, employers, insurers, public utilities, and others purchase your credit report to make decisions to grant you loans, jobs, insurance, and other products or services. This report cannot be given to these establishments or individuals without your signed authorization. When signing an application for a job, loan, or lease on an apartment, you normally find a clause outlining the use of your information, which states that they have the right to perform a credit check on you prior to going ahead with an agreement.

Having a low credit score can be detrimental in obtaining some of the necessities of life, such as a job, an apartment, a credit card, or a mortgage. A low score could also cause your finance charges to be increased due to you being considered a higher risk.

Having a poor credit record can be quite inconvenient as it can follow you for several years. Those late payments and other derogatory issues can remain on your credit report for as long as seven years and a bankruptcy can remain on your record for up to ten years. This is why it is really important to keep your debts up to date and paid on time as well as ensuring that the debts on your credit report are really yours and not the work of a fraudster.

Consumers with excellent credit usually receive better interest rates from most lenders. Those who show good credit behavior usually have no problem securing credit when they need it. The credit score, however, is only one component of a lender's criteria for approving loans. Other factors could include your income, length of employment, and other debts that you need to service. If there are other debts on your credit report that don't belong to you, you need to correct that immediately.

What Does a Credit Report Look Like?

Understanding the components of a credit report is important if you need to review it for accuracy. The first component of the report is the personal section that outlines the following items: your name, Social Insurance Number (SIN), date of birth, marital status, current and former addresses, and the name of your past and current employer(s). If you had a former name, that may be included as well.

Another part of the credit report is the section that covers public records such as previous loan defaults, bankruptcies, and any other legal judgements against you.

A very important section is the credit history section, which include items such as installment credit (loans with a specific payment amount and payment period), revolving credit accounts (credit cards and lines of credit), the date each account was opened, the credit limits or loan amounts, the balances, and the monthly payments. This section will also show if you are on time or late with your payments, indicating how many days late. All current and old accounts are included in this section of the credit report. Additional information provides details of your credit transactions and show whether payments are being made as agreed.

The credit grantor evaluates each of these items. Evaluations are based on industry standard ratings, which use a range from R0 to R9. R0 indicates you are too new to rate; R1 indicates that you pay within thirty days of billing or as agreed; R9 indicates a bad debt, collection, or bankruptcy. R2 indicates you are paying between thirty and sixty days, and R3 sixty to ninety days, and so on. Any payment past thirty days is an indication of slow payment history and is not considered favourably by the lenders or those granting contracts such as leases or phones. If you had only one or two R2s, you could be okay, but if you had many R2s that were recent and a few R3s and higher, you may have difficulty obtaining the credit or contract. Most thieves who steal your identity and set up credit in your name usually don't pay the debt off, so the R1 turns to an R9 very quickly. This is another good reason to review your credit reports annually.

The last section is the "Inquiries" area that lists any creditors, insurance companies, and lenders who have requested your credit report. As mentioned earlier, these companies or individuals may not inquire about your credit information without your prior consent. Each inquiry made by these groups causes a "hard" inquiry to be recorded on your file.

Multiple hard inquiries will have an impact on your credit rating. Should you be declined by a lender, understand why and what action you can take to correct your credit situation rather than going from lender to lender. When you personally make an inquiry through one of the three reporting credit bureaus, it is not considered a hard inquiry and will not affect your score or rating.

Credit reports do not include information unrelated to credit, such as race, gender, religion, national origin, personal lifestyle, political preference, and driving records. A credit bureau doesn't disclose medical information and will not contain information about your chequing and savings accounts or investment accounts. Conventional mortgages do not appear on the credit bureau, though financial institutions are in discussion about disclosing this information to the bureaus.

Your Credit Score

All the information in your credit report is used to calculate your credit score. The credit score, which can range between 300 and 850, summarizes your creditworthiness. The score assists potential lenders, landlords, and employers to quickly gauge your credit behaviour. The score may predict how likely you are to make your credit payments on time and may be used to assist in evaluating you for a potential job. Risk is a major determining factor behind lending and the score assists in measuring risk. If you've been a victim of identity theft and you were not aware of the poor credit score due to this breach, you could be denied a job or a loan as a result.

The scoring models may vary from agency to agency, but they are all influenced by the same two items: how you pay your debts and how much debt you owe. The score is formulated with close attention to the following details:

• Your payment history. Do you pay on time? Do you have bankruptcies or other negative items on your record, such as a late payment history?

- What is the total debt owed? Are you up to the limit on any of your accounts?
- How long is your credit history? Do you demonstrate responsible credit management?
- New credit activity. Did you recently apply for or open new credit accounts?

The average person usually has a credit score in the 600s and 700s. A score above 700 is a sign of financial health and may earn you favourable lending terms. In some cases, there are credit score thresholds required to qualify for specific types of mortgages and home-equity lines of credit (HELOC). You may need a higher credit score to get a revolving line of credit like the HELOC than you would a conventional fixed-rate mortgage, as the revolving line has a higher risk for the lender. The conventional fixed-rate mortgage doesn't carry as much of a risk because it has a declining balance. The revolving line could be at its limit for the life of the loan, which could create more risk and in turn would require a better credit score to properly manage. Depending on the type of loan and the associated risks, your credit score can be a significant deciding factor on whether you qualify.

Credit scores below 600 will be viewed as high risk and lenders may turn down credit applicants with those kinds of scores. A low score may force you to use a "sub-prime" lender, who may offer you less favourable payment terms such as higher interest rates. In addition, you may have to make a larger down payment if buying a house. In Canada, the sub-prime lending business has recently opened up to lots of competition. The sub-prime market was set up to cover the void left by the larger lenders who didn't have the products to meet the borrowers' needs. Some of the larger financial institutions have set up sub-prime lending through affiliated companies or referral arrangements.

Please note that each spouse has a separate score that reflects his or her own past credit history and you do not share a credit score.

How Can I Obtain a Copy of My Credit Report or Credit Score?

We recommend that you review your credit report at least annually so you can review changes to your credit profile to confirm the accuracy and completeness of information that is being reported. By reviewing your credit report, you can see if anyone has stolen your identity and opened credit in your name. We recommend you review your credit report before you plan to make a major purchase so that you can correct any errors. Correcting errors can assist you in maintaining a higher credit score and getting better credit terms.

Remember that you have more than just one credit file. Most likely, each of the three major consumer credit bureaus (Equifax, TransUnion, and Northern Credit Bureaus [Experian]) has a report on you. You must request your credit report; this is not a service that is provided to you automatically. And remember that checking your own credit report won't cause a "hard inquiry" to be recorded. In other words, it will not diminish your credit score like frequent credit checks by financial institutions could.

Obtaining a Free Credit Report

In order to request your free credit report by mail from one of the three credit bureaus, simply follow the steps outlined on their respective websites. In all cases, you are required to send the completed and signed form to their offices with proof of identification. The identification must include government-issued photo ID as well as other ID that supports your name, date of birth, and signature. To review these steps, please go to their websites:

TransUnion: www.transunion.ca
Equifax: www.equifax.ca
Northern Credit Bureaus (Experian):
   www.creditbureau.ca

Acceptable Primary Identification
   In order to issue a report, credit bureaus require one piece
of valid, non-expired Canadian Government–issued identification. Examples include:

- Driver's license
- Canadian passport
- Certificate of Indian Status (CIS)
- Birth certificate
- Permanent Resident card (PR Card)
- Citizenship and immigration form
- Health card (excluding the provinces of Ontario, Manitoba, and Prince Edward Island)
- Old Age Security (OAS) identification card
- Department of National Defence card

Additional Pieces of Acceptable Identification
   Examples include:

- Utility bill indicating current address (within sixty days of issue)
- Credit card statement indicating current address (within sixty days of issue)
- Signed credit card
- CNIB card
- Social insurance card
- T4 slip (current tax year)
- Notice of Assessments (current tax year)
- GST/HST refunds (current tax year)
- Child tax benefits (current tax year)

Together, these combined pieces must contain your name, current address, date of birth, and signature.

If you don't want to wait for the report via mail, all three credit bureaus will send one to you electronically at a nominal fee. Again, the instructions and fees are outlined on their respective websites.

What If My Credit Report Contains Inaccurate Information?

Once you receive your copy of your credit report, it is important that you review it for accuracy. There may be errors in the report that may cause your score to be inaccurate, which in turn may cause you to be denied credit, a job, a lease, or even a telephone account. You should look at the inquiry section to see if each inquiry belongs to you. If someone has made an inquiry without your consent, it could potentially be fraud.

You may have accounts opened that need to be closed if they are no longer in use. You should also verify that your payment history is up to date. If someone has reported a slow payment history that is inaccurate, you may want to correct that as well.

You have the right to dispute any errors you find in your credit report. As soon as you find an error or incomplete information, you should contact the credit reporting agencies to advise them of the error immediately. You should follow the instructions on the report or their websites so you can resolve any issues in a prompt manner. It is highly recommended that you keep records of all written and oral communications as well as copies of any pertinent data such as receipts, sales slips, and bank or credit card statements. We recommend that you send all correspondence via registered mail with signature required upon receipt.

Most creditors update credit bureau information monthly and it is possible that incorrect information could be removed and then added back as the creditor could be pending an update. In order to review your report for accuracy after an error has been corrected, you should check after sixty days to see if the correction is up to date.

The credit bureaus do not change information in your credit report unless it is shown to be incomplete or inaccurate. If you dispute something, the credit bureaus ask their source to verify the information. If that fails to resolve the question in your favour, you can write a short statement that the credit bureau can add to your file.

If you are a victim of identity theft, you can request that the credit bureaus insert an alert on your credit report so that any further credit requests will be handled with caution. This will make it a little more difficult to borrow money because you will have to make an extra effort to prove your identity each time. It's worth it because you may be stopping fraud and preventing someone from tarnishing your name.

You Can Improve Your Credit Score

Your credit score is not static and it changes when your information changes at the credit-reporting agency. The following are some guidelines on how you can improve your score over time:

- Pay all of your bills and loans on time.
- If you are unable to pay your bills or loans on time, contact your creditor immediately to work out a payment plan.
- Refrain from applying for credit at a multitude of places to avoid excessive inquiries. A large number of inquiries over a short period of time might be interpreted as you being a credit seeker, which could mean that you are opening numerous accounts due to financial difficulty or maybe you are overextending yourself.
- Only maintain the credit cards you really need and use—

the fewer, the better.
- Close all unused credit accounts.
- Be reasonable with your debts and keep your credit balances as low as possible. A good rule of thumb is not to exceed 50% of your card or line of credit limit.
- Only apply for new accounts when you need them.
- Correct any inaccuracies on your credit report immediately so you have the true score on file. Incorrect reports will have a lower than normal score.

Identity thieves have the power to hijack your life when they open accounts in your name. It is really important that you review your credit report annually to ensure you aren't being victimized.

Credit Monitoring
In addition to getting an annual report from one of the credit bureaus, you can also sign up, for a nominal fee, for a credit monitoring service that will quickly alert you to any changes in your profile. The one offered by TransUnion is currently $22.95 per quarter and it provides:

- Weekly e-mail alerts that keep you informed about credit profile changes and potential fraud,
- Quarterly online access to your credit profile with analytical tools, and
- Unlimited toll-free access to credit specialists.

They also offer additional monitoring of your score and debts for $7.95 each per quarter. By the time you are finished, you could be spending over $155 per year to receive a complete up-to-date report on your credit report, credit score, and debts on a quarterly and even daily basis for some components of this service. Do you really need this service? Some may say yes and some may go for the annual report review instead. It all depends on your own personal preferences.

Identity Theft Protection

There are a few identity-theft protection companies operating in Canada that provide various related services. For example, Pre-Paid Legal Care of Canada currently offers a plan for $12.95 per month. They suggest a three step plan:

- Protect your identity,
- Quarterly consumer credit disclosure, learn of suspicious activity early, and monitor your information, and
- Identity restoration, a trained expert will take the steps to restore your name and credit for you.

Ralph Vandervoort, Certified Financial Planner of V Group Financial, recently told us that he strongly recommends this service to his clients as it offers peace of mind and protection against identity theft. This is also a great service for seniors who want to protect their assets and name. It's quite similar to buying title insurance on your home. We will cover that topic in greater detail in Chapter 5: Mortgage and Title Fraud.

Credit Repair

There are many companies popping up due to the growth of identity theft. As a consumer, you should be cautious of where you spend your money to protect your identity and your financial well-being. One type of business that has started soliciting consumers is the credit repair company. They make promises to clean up or erase your bad credit and even give you a fresh start. They usually charge high fees and may not deliver on their promises or agreements with you. Before you think of hiring someone else to repair or fix your credit, remember this:

- There are no loopholes or laws that credit repair companies can use to get correct information off your credit report.
- You can do the same thing the credit repair company can do yourself.

- No one can require a credit bureau to remove accurate negative information before the legal time frame is up.
- The only way to repair bad credit is with good credit practices over a period of time.

As you go through your routine of applying for loans, mortgages, jobs, and other activities that require an application of some kind, please take note that an inquiry will be made, in most cases, for a credit report on you. If that report is accurate, you should have no problems at all, but if there are some skeletons in the closet, make sure you do some housekeeping as quickly as possible to protect your name and your financial well-being. Again, we recommend you review your credit annually—or more often if you desire—and check for any inaccuracies.

Chapter 4

Internet and E-Mail Fraud

Internet-related scams can cause an enormous amount of damage and they can be very overwhelming for anybody who gets caught up in one of them. Given the variety of viruses, combined with the level of sophistication by which your privacy can be violated, simply opening an e-mail can be a nightmare. For most people, the world of Internet viruses, spam, and fraud can make the World Wide Web unsafe at any speed. Con artists have gone high-tech just like everyone else. Fraudsters are using the Internet to defraud consumers, using e-mail to reach millions of people.

Con artists are trying all of their old scams but with an electronic twist. They are hijacking consumers' modems and computers so they can ring up hefty long-distance charges on their phone bills.

Spyware, unknown by many consumers, is used by marketers to track your Web traffic and it can sneak onto your computer's hard drive without your consent or knowledge when you are innocently surfing the Internet. Spyware is the same software that generates the annoying pop-up messages and advertisements. These pop-ups are notorious for continuously interfering with your ability to browse online.

Unknown unauthorized software that gets onto your hard drive to track your movements is invasive. The disturbing thing about this breech of privacy is the fact that your personal activities on the Internet could get into the wrong hands and could be used for less-than-honourable intentions.

There are people who design viruses for a living and they do so with the intent on causing major damage to your personal computer as well as those computers and systems in the corporate and government environment. One such way of accessing your computer is through the use of spoofing, which is currently on an upward trend. Hackers (those who perform these malicious acts) send e-mail to thousands or even millions of people with a message that appears to be from someone else.

When they send the deceptive e-mail, they hide their true identity—this is how we get the name "spoofing." The virus is usually hidden inside the e-mail in an attachment or a link to a website.

Internet scammers are using many tricks to deceive you and this goes beyond the spoofing. These hackers are trying very hard to gain access to your personal information as well as your banking and credit card information. They are casting about in many ways to lure you into their nets. This practice of luring you into disclosing your personal information is known as phishing. We will cover more on spoofing and phishing throughout this chapter.

Thanks to the Internet, we now have access to information, entertainment, products, and financial services from all over the world. The generations before us never would have imagined the access we have today.

You can now do so many things online, including access e-mail from any computer; order any product, ranging from a toaster to a book; download music or games; reserve a hotel, car, or plane ticket; and check your bank or credit card balances 24 hours a day. On the flip side of all this, the Internet can give the criminals access to your computer and all of its content and activity.

To ensure safety while using the Internet, you need to adopt safe practices so you can minimize the chances of online scammers, hackers, and identity thieves from gaining control of your personal information, closing down your computer or hijacking it completely.

Phishing and Spoofing

Phishing and spoofing are quite similar in that they refer to forged or faked electronic documents.

Phishing is a high-tech scam that uses spam and/or pop-up messages to deceive consumers into disclosing their card numbers, bank account information, social insurance numbers, passwords, or other confidential and personal information. According to the Anti-Phishing Working Group (APWG) (an international organization committed to wiping out Internet scams and fraud), the word "phishing" comes from the analogy that Internet scammers are using e-mail lures to "fish" for passwords and financial data from the sea of Internet users.

It is not unusual for an Internet "phisher" to send deceptive e-mails or pop-up messages that claim to be from a business or organization that you normally deal with. Examples of these types of groups include your Internet service provider (ISP), financial institution, or even a government agency. These organizations would never send you an e-mail requesting personal or confidential information, so you should be very cautious and wary when opening up these e-mails. Never provide any information, even if they say they need it to update or validate your accounts.

The malicious e-mail might threaten some horrible outcome if you don't respond or it may direct you to visit a "spoofed" website. These fake websites often look just like the legitimate organization's site. The purpose of the phony site is to trick you into revealing your personal information so the fraudsters can steal your identity, steal your assets, empty your bank accounts or commit crimes in your name.

Spoofing is where the fraudster creates a false or shadow copy of a real website or e-mail in a way that misleads the recipient. The spoofer's computer captures all of the network traffic on the victim's browser, which allows the spoofer to acquire confidential information such as credit card numbers, passwords, and bank account numbers. The e-mail and website look very authentic with all the right logos, colours, and even telephone numbers that have an answering service.

The slick phishers and spoofers are getting better and better at what they do. They can put a fake website on top of the real site so they can capture your inputted information as you key it in on the legitimate site. As soon as you provide them with the personal information, they will most likely sell it to other criminals who in turn use it to access your credit cards or bank accounts. The underground market for this data is enormous and internationally practiced.

The APWG is building a repository of phishing scam e-mails and websites to help people identify and avoid being scammed in the future. If you have received a phishing e-mail and would like to submit it to APWG, please send it to reportphishing@antiphishing.org. They will review the message and any websites to which it links and post it to the Phishing Archive on their site. Here are instructions for submitting phishing e-mail, assuming you use Outlook or Netscape:

• Create a new e-mail to reportphishing@antiphishing.org.
• Drag and drop the phishing e-mail from your inbox onto this new e-mail message. In Netscape, drop it on the "attachment" area.
• Do not use "forward" if you can help it, as this approach

loses information and requires more manual processing. The exception is when you use the Web interface to Outlook; in that case, forward is the only solution.

Mike's Story

Mike lives in Montreal and is a retired government employee. Mike had recently installed up-to-date antivirus software and a firewall on his computer. He knows not to click on an attachment in an e-mail if he wasn't expecting it, and he knew that this precaution applied to e-mail from friends as well as unidentified senders.

One day, Mike received an e-mail that appeared to come from his bank, asking him to logon to his banking and investment account to update his personal information. He clicked on the URL in the e-mail and went directly to his bank's website—or so it seemed. In reality, the URL in the e-mail took Mike to a look-a-like website. The site looked identical to his own bank site, so when he was asked for his account number, username, and password, he automatically started to type them in. Then he remembered something he had heard at a talk given at his local Rotary Club approximately two months before.

The featured speaker talked about phishing attacks, specifically mentioning look-a-like websites. The key to recognizing them, Mike remembered, was that a bank would never send its customers an e-mail with a link in it asking customers to click and log in to their account. "If you receive such an e-mail," the speaker said, "simply discard it." So he did.

Mike had just been the latest intended victim of the very thing he'd recently heard about: a phishing attack. However, he remembered just in time the simple rule that a bank would never send a web link asking for personal information via e-mail. Had he entered the information he was asked for, the cybercriminals would have everything they needed to manipulate his banking and investment account.[9]

Phishing Expedition

Here is another example of phishing. This e-mail was received on one of our own personal e-mail accounts and you can be sure that this isn't the only time it's been received. The e-mail is full of spelling errors, and that is a common pattern you will find with many of the international scams on the e-mail spam circuit. This particular case involves a common theme: "You have won something but we need some personal information to give you your prize." In some instances, they will even ask for money up front before they send you your prize—this is commonly referred to as advance-fee fraud.

YAHOO MAIL AWARD WINNING NOTIFICATION
From the desk of the Email Promotions Manager, International Promotions/Prize Award Department, Yahoo.co.uk
3b Olympic Way, Sefton Business Park, Aintree, Liverpool, L30 1RD

Ref:No:YH-L/200-26937 Batch: 2007YJL-01

We are pleased to inform you of the announcement today of winners of the YAHOO MEGA JACKPOT LOTTO WINNINGS PROGRAMS held on 10th FEBRUARY 2007.

Your company or your personal email address is attached to winning number 20-12FEB-2007-02YAHOO, with serial number S/N-00168 drew the lucky numbers 887-13-865-37-10-83, and consequently won in the first lottery category.

You have therefore been approved for a lump sum pay out of GBP 2,500,000.00 POUNDS in cash. This is from total prize money of GBP 27,500,000.00 POUNDS, shared among the Twenty (5) international winners in this category. This cash will be credited to file Ref No: Yahoo-L/200-26937.

All participants were selected through our YAHOO computer ballot system drawn form 21,000 names,3,000 names from each continent, as part of International "EMAIL" Promotions Program, which is conducted annually for our prominent YAHOO user all over the world, and for the continues use of Email.

Your fund has been deposited in an escrow account and in-sured with your REF NO: YH-L/200-26937 and your Email address, Please note that, you are to contact us via email and not phone as we are promoting the use of Email, any com-munications with this office should be by mail, You have the right to call the bank, as we will provide you with the neces-sary details on how to claim your prize.

You are to keep your ref. number and batch number from the public, until you have been processed and your money re-mitted to your account. This is part of our security protocol to avoid double claiming and the act and scamming people of their reference number and prizes. We hope with a part of your prize, you will participate in our year high stakes US$1.3 BILLION International Lottery.

To claim your winning prize, you must first contact the claims department by email for processing and remittance of your prize money to you.

The claims officer contact email is:
Name: Mrs. Susan Anthony
Email:susananthony10@yahoo.co.uk

AND PLEASE NOTE THAT YOU ARE TO SEND THE BELOW INFORMATIONS REQUIRED TO CLAIM YOUR WINNING PRIZE:

1. FULL NAMES: _____
2. NATIONALITY: _____
3. DATE OF BIRTH _____
4. SEX: _____
5. MARITAL STATUS:_____
6. CONTACT ADDRESS:_____
7. TELEPHONE NUMBER:_____
8. OCCUPATION:_____
9. WINNINGEMAIL ADDRESS:_____
10. REF/BATCH NUMBERS:_____
11. TOTAL AMOUNT WON:_____

Upon receipt of the duly requested data, i`ll send you the contact information of the payment office so you can proceed with effecting the release of your claim in anyway you deem fit, summit back immediately.

NOTE: In order to avoid unnecessary delays and complications, please remember to quote your reference and batch numbers in all correspondences with your claims officer. Do not reply any other mails like this on net as they are alot of scam artist out there pretending to be us. You may see mails like this do not reply. Do contact your claims officer Mrs.Susan Anthony at once by email. You will be asked to provide some details to enable us proceed file keeping.

PLEASE KEEP THIS CONFIDENTIAL.
Sincerely,
Mr.Henry Sills

For YAHOO LOTTO UK;
NOTE: Do not reply this mail. You are to contact your claims officer immediately.

SPONSORS:

CHIEF SPONSOR;
YAHOO,YAHOO.CO.UK
COOPERATIONS ASIA YAHOO
CO-OPERATIONSUSA
!!!!!!!CONGRATULATIONS!!!!!!!

Here are a few comments on this e-mail:

• Yahoo! does not send out award notifications. If you win a prize of some kind, you will be notified by the company hosting the contest.
• If you never entered this contest, how could you win?
• Yahoo! does not run lotteries.
• The e-mail is a spoof that is attempting to extract personal information from you, which is a true form of phishing.

Remember, at no time will a bank ever ask you to provide information to them in such a way. Here is an example of one such fraudulent e-mail:

Dear RBC Customer:

We recently have determined that different computers have logged into your Rbc Online Banking account, and multiple password failures were present before the logons. We now need you to log into your account and verify your account activity. We have issued this warning message.

It has come to our attention that your Rcb Bank account information needs to be reactivated as part of our continuing commitment to protect your account and to reduce the instance of fraud on our website in this new Season. Once you have reactivated your account records your Rbc Online Banking account service will not be interrupted and will continue as normal.

To reactivate your Rbc account records click on the following link:

http://www.rbc.com/signon?LOB=reactivateAcct

Accounts Management As outlined in our User Agreement, RBC Royal will periodically send you information about site changes and enhancements.

Visit our Privacy Policy and User Agreement if you have any questions. http://www.rbc.com/help /index.jhtml

Take note of the spelling errors and how they use a well-known bank's name to phish you in. They even have a website that could have a virus or be a front to steal your personal information. Never open any links on any of these fake e-mails or go to their fake sites.

Tips to Avoiding Phishing Scams

As a general rule, online banking and shopping online is quite safe, but you should be careful about giving out your personal financial information over the Internet. The Anti-Phishing Working Group (APWG) is the global pan-indus-trial and law enforcement association focused on eliminating the fraud and identity theft that result from phishing, pharm-ing, and e-mail spoofing of all types. Here is a list of tips on how to avoid phishing scams from their website, www.antiphishing.org:

• Be suspicious of any e-mail with urgent requests for per-sonal financial information. The e-mail may include up-setting or exciting (but false) statements to get you to react immediately and will ask for information such as usernames, passwords, credit card numbers, social insur-ance numbers, etc.

- Don't use the links in an e-mail to get to any web page. Instead, call the company on the telephone or access the website directly by typing in the web address in your browser.

- If you need to update your information online, use the normal process you've used before or open a new browser window and type in the website address of the legitimate company's account maintenance page.

- If a website address is unfamiliar, it's probably not real. Only use the address that you have used before or start at your normal homepage.

- Avoid filling out forms in e-mail messages that ask for personal financial information.

- Always ensure that you're using a secure website when submitting credit card or other sensitive information via your web browser.

- Most companies require you to log in to a secure site. Look for the lock symbol at the bottom of your browser and "https" in front of the website address. Both of these indicate that you are in a secure and encrypted area.

- Take note of the header address on the website. Most legitimate sites will have a relatively short Internet address that usually depicts the business name followed by ".com" or possibly ".org." Spoof sites are more likely to have an excessively long string of characters in the header, with the legitimate business name somewhere in the string, or possibly not at all.

- Regularly log into your online accounts.

- Regularly check your bank, credit, and debit card statements to be sure that there are no unauthorized transactions. If anything looks suspicious, contact your bank and all card issuers.

- Ensure that your browser is up to date and security patches have been applied. Do the same with your computer's operating system and antivirus software.

- Always report fraudulent or suspicious e-mails. Reporting instances of spoofed websites will help get them shut down before they can do any more harm.

- If you have any doubts about an e-mail or website, contact the legitimate company directly. Make a copy of the questionable website's URL address and send it to the legitimate business to ask if the request is legitimate.

Keystroke Logging

Keystroke logging comes from malicious software, which is sometimes called malware. Malicious software is designed to monitor or influence computer behaviour. It can be found in different forms, such as viruses, worms, Trojan horse programs, spyware, and adware. Computers can become infected with malicious software by opening e-mail, accessing a website, using infected media, or downloading and running infected programs. The malicious code may capture personal information from your computer or keyboard. This confidential and personal information would then be transmitted to the criminal. One method is by logging your keystrokes. Keystroke loggers come in two varieties: small hardware devices or a software program, and both do the same thing.

Hardware keystroke loggers are tiny devices that sit between the keyboard and the computer. They are available for as little as $100 and some models are indistinguishable from a standard keyboard plug. In order for the criminal to set up a hardware keystroke logger, they must have access to the back of your computer. This hardware device will sit there and record up to a year's worth of typing. When the fraudster is ready to retrieve the data, they can either remove the device and take it to their own machine or simply download the information to disk directly from the target machine, leaving the device in place to capture more unsuspecting victims.

Software keystroke loggers are more ideal since it is very difficult to install a hardware keystroke logger on a home PC. The software keystroke logger is an invisible program that once installed and activated runs in the background on your computer secretly recording every key you hit and storing the results in a hidden file. The criminals usually access the keystroke information remotely, but they could also access it locally depending on the type of software they are using. The software to gain this information and perform these tasks is readily available on the Internet. Some people and organizations actually use this software to monitor their children's Internet activity or an employee's computer behaviour.

Key Logging Victim

John works as a writer for a local newspaper and lives in the suburbs of a large city. He has used a computer in his job for more than six years. His computer at work is maintained by his company's IT department, and he has never experienced any security problems with the computer in his office.

John considers himself to be computer savvy and believes that he is at low risk of online fraud for the following reasons:

- He never shops online because he doesn't want to risk exposing his credit card information, and he doesn't like the idea that data about his purchases might be stored and used to make a profile of his likes and dislikes.

- He only uses his home computer for personal e-mail with friends and family, to surf the web for information about new developments in his field, and to do banking once a month via his bank's website.
- He occasionally looks other things up on the web, but not often.

John's situation seems safe enough, right?

Unfortunately, looks can be deceiving. At work one day last summer, he heard about a new Internet Explorer browser vulnerability; it was so critical that emergency patches for all work computers in his organization had been distributed by his IT department that same day. He wanted to be sure his home computer was protected, too, so when he got home, he went online to get more information about the vulnerability and determine if he was protected.

Using a popular search engine, he found a website that offered information about the vulnerability in addition to the option of having a patch downloaded automatically to his computer. John read the information, but opted not to accept the download since he was taught to download information only from authorized sources. Then he went to the official Microsoft site to obtain the patch.

So, what went wrong?

Unfortunately, as John was reading information about the vulnerability on the first site, the criminal who had created the Website was taking advantage of the fact his computer actually had the vulnerability. Actually, as he was clicking "No" to refuse the download that was being offered, unbeknownst to him, the automatic installation of a small but powerful crimeware program was already taking place on his computer.

The program was a keystroke logger. Within seconds of John's clicking, the website's owner began receiving notification that the keystroke logger had been secretly and successfully installed on John's computer. The program was designed to secretly log everything he typed in from that moment on, and to send all of the information to the website owner as well. It functioned flawlessly, too, recording everything John typed, every website he visited, and every e-mail he sent, passing the stolen text on to the cybercriminal.

Later that evening, John finished up his monthly online banking. As he logged into his personal bank account, the keystroke logger recorded those keystrokes, too, including confidential information: the name of his bank, his user ID, his password, the last four digits of his Social Insurance Number, and his mother's maiden name. The bank's system was secure, and all the data he typed in was encrypted so no one along the route could casually interpret the information. However, the key-logging program was recording the information in real time—as he typed it in and before it was encrypted—allowing it to bypass the security that was in place.

It was just a matter of time before John's crucial banking information was in the hands of a criminal. His name, and all of the associated information, was added to a long list of names of other unsuspecting users and sold to someone the criminal had met on the Internet—someone specialized in using stolen bank information to make illegal withdrawals. When John went to make a deposit several weeks later and asked for his balance statement, he was shocked to find that his bank account was almost empty. He had been the victim of a cybercrime.[10]

How to Protect Yourself from Keystroke Loggers
* Make sure your system is up to date. Regularly update your system with all available patches and security updates, as this will take care of newly discovered vulnerabilities.

* Lock down your software. Your web browser and e-mail

are the two most vulnerable areas. You should turn off the automatic preview feature in your e-mail client. Read all pop-up warnings carefully. If you are not expecting to install a program or if you aren't sure what the program does, don't click the cancel button. Instead, close the window immediately by clicking the small square "x" in the top right corner.

- Don't be promiscuous. You should never download or accept files from people or websites you're not sure about. It's only a matter of time before you get infected if you practice indiscriminate downloading.

- Get protection. Having a good antivirus package is only a part of the solution. It is extremely important that you update your antivirus protection on a regular basis so you can deal with new viruses that are being released all the time.

- Beware of e-mail attachments. You should never open an e-mail attachment unless you know where it's coming from or you have verified that it is truly coming from that person. Always verify if an attachment is unexpected. Many viruses spread by infected e-mails. Viruses send themselves to contacts in the e-mail address book.

- More protection. It is strongly recommended that you run a spyware detector and a firewall. Both of these are available, either free or at a low cost. The firewall is useful in alerting you of harmful software.

File Sharing and Free Software

Millions of computer users are sharing files on a regular basis so they can access a wealth of information such as music, videos, games, and software. When you access these files, you are connecting to an informal network of other computers that are running the same software. Millions of users could be connected at the same time as you.

There are risks associated with file sharing, and in most cases, the software is free and easy to access. To minimize the risks and your exposure, check the program settings before you download any free software. Some software may have other motives, including accessing personal information on your hard drive such as e-mail messages, photos, or other documents that you don't want to share. The "End User License Agreement" usually outlines what the software license permits at your end as well as theirs. If you are willing to put up with the side effects of the free downloads, it's okay to proceed; however, if you are not sure, remove the software completely through the proper uninstall process. Be cautious when downloading material as some items may be protected by copyright.

Spam

When someone sends spam over the Internet, they are sending unsolicited bulk e-mail. "Unsolicited" means the recipient never gave verifiable permission for the e-mail to be sent. "Bulk" means the e-mail message was sent as part of a larger group of e-mails with very similar content. Due to technological advances and the growing use of the Internet, spam is a very popular tool for committing crimes such as fraud and identity theft.

Spam has grown to the point where it is causing so much e-mail traffic that it is hurting legitimate e-commerce of all kinds. It is being used to violate computers and networks worldwide on a daily basis as it accesses computers and servers without authorization and transmits malicious codes and viruses.

The Problem

Industry Canada recently stated:

> In just a few years, [spam] has gone from being a minor nuisance to becoming a significant social and economic issue, and a drain on the business and personal productivity of Canadians [...]. Spam now impedes the efficient use of e-mail for personal and business communications, and threatens the growth and acceptance of legitimate e-commerce.[11]

Here are some additional points of interest from the Industry Canada findings:

- In the year 2000, e-mail traffic reports indicated that spam amounted to about 10% of the total volume of e-mail.
- By 2002, the percentage of spam e-mail had climbed to 30%.
- In early 2003, tracking services recorded a dubious milestone: the amount of unsolicited commercial e-mail had surpassed that of legitimate communications.
- By the end of 2004, it was predicted that spam constituted as much as 70% of global e-mail.
- Spam e-mail traffic is estimated to account for approximately 80% of all e-mail traffic.

To Internet service providers, or anyone who provides facilities for the Internet services, the cost to manage spam is climbing with the volume of these unsolicited bulk e-mails. These costs are being passed on to organizations and consumers who use the Internet for electronic communications. Spam is also undermining the reliability of e-mail as it threatens consumer confidence in doing business on the Internet (i.e. e-commerce).

We all thought that communication technology would bolster productivity; now it is being constrained by all the spam. There is no doubt that e-mail is efficient, but when over 80% of it is garbage, you start to get tired of taking out the trash.

Everyone should play a role in stopping spam. Consumers, lawmakers, enforcement agencies, ISPs, and other network operators all need to work together to fight spam. All Internet end-users need to be vigilant, and by doing so, we can contribute to a reduction in spam. Internet users need to be aware of all the available tools that can be used to limit the amount of spam they receive. Education can play a big role in protecting you from spam and all the garbage it delivers. When you open an e-mail or an attachment that was sent as spam, you are now alerting the messenger that your e-mail address is good and active. The floodgates are now open!

"Do not open unsolicited e-mails," "Do not buy from spammers," and "Do not provide personal information if you are not certain who you are dealing with" are some of the simplest warnings, but either they haven't reached all users or they haven't been understood. For example, the Ipsos-Reid *Ipsos Trend Report Canada* for May–June 2004 reported that more than one third of online Canadians open their spam e-mails, and that the main reason they give for doing so is curiosity.

A recent study by Option Consommateurs indicated that certain groups might benefit from increased education and awareness efforts tailored to their specific needs. These groups include people under thirty—who reported receiving more spam than other groups—and the elderly.

Three Key Tips to Stop Spam
1) Protect your computer. Since spam is a growing source of computer viruses, we recommend you protect your computer from virus-carrying messages by installing and regularly updating antivirus and anti-spam software. We also recommend the extra protection of a firewall.

2) Protect your e-mail address. Use one e-mail for your trusted personal and business contacts. Set up a separate e-mail address for other online uses.

3) Protect yourself. Delete spam as soon as you see it on your computer. Don't try, don't buy, and don't reply to spam. It prevents receiving more spam in the future.

Each of us must try do our part to protect ourselves and others from spam and all the problems this e-mail delivers.

Canada's Office of Consumer Affairs, part of Industry Canada, created a great spam IQ test to provide you with the opportunity to find out how much you know about spam and to learn how to better protect yourself. The results you get at the end of the test can also provide you with new ways to protect yourself, your computer, and your e-mail address. Making the Internet a safer place is in everyone's interest. The spam IQ test is available at the following website:

http://strategis.ic.gc.ca/epic/site/oca-bc.nsf/en/ca02141e.html

And remember, don't try, don't buy, and don't reply to spam. Just delete it.

Wireless Technology

As Internet traffic and technology develop, so does the need to eliminate the wires that connect all the computers. Wireless networks (often called Wi-Fi) are becoming extremely popular. They allow computers to connect to one another without cables. Using radio technology comparable to cordless phones, they make it easy to connect to networks, e-mail, and the Internet. Regrettably, they also make it easy for outsiders to do the same. Any information travelling on airways through Wi-Fi could be at risk of being intercepted by anyone who has the equipment to perform such an interception.

Computer users are accessing the Internet wirelessly because they are interested in convenience and mobility. The Wi-Fi revolution is extremely strong and growing at a fast rate with many homes and businesses setting up networks. More than ever, business travellers use wireless devices to stay in touch with their workplace, family, and friends. It's not unusual to receive pictures from a friend while they are still on vacation or to buy something from another part of the world from the comfort of your couch. Setting up a wireless network at your home or office is very simple and it is without the tangle of cards and cables.

Numerous computers in many parts of your home or office can connect to the network as long as they are in the network's range. If you want to set up a wireless network, you will require a broadband Internet connection to your home or office called an "access point." This access point could be a cable or DSL line that runs into the modem. Once you have the access point, you need to connect to a wireless router that sends (broadcasts) a signal through the air. This signal can travel as far as several hundred feet depending on the location of the access point and wireless router. Any computer within range of the signal that is equipped with a wireless card can gain access to the Internet on your network.

From a security standpoint, this easy access is the downside of the wireless network, so you need to take precautions to prevent strangers from accessing your Internet connection. If you don't take precautions, you could be letting complete strangers on your network, and if they are criminal-minded, they could gain access to your personal information. When someone uses your connection and they commit a crime or go to a website that isn't considered suitable, it will appear as though you did the crime or visited that particular website. There have been cases where people have been arrested for committing a crime on their computers, but when the investigations were completed, law enforcement agencies have been able to identify hackers as the criminals and not the innocent users.

There are some steps you can take to protect your wireless network and the computers on it. Taking all of the following steps will help you be more secure.[12]

1) Use encryption. The most effective way to secure your wireless network from intruders is to encrypt, or scramble, communications over the network. Most wireless routers, access points, and base stations have a built-in encryption mechanism. If your wireless router doesn't have an encryption feature, consider getting one that does. Manufacturers often deliver wireless routers with the encryption feature turned off. You must turn it on. The directions that come with your wireless router should explain how to do that. If they don't, check the router manufacturer's website. Two main types of encryption are available: Wi-Fi Protected Access (WPA) and Wired Equivalent Privacy (WEP). Your computer, router, and other equipment must use the same encryption. WPA is stronger; use it if you have a choice. It should protect you against most hackers. Some older routers use only WEP encryption, which is better than no encryption. It should protect your wireless network against accidental intrusions by neighbours or attacks by less-sophisticated hackers. If you use WEP encryption, set it to the highest security level available.

2) Use antivirus and anti-spyware software, and a firewall. Computers on a wireless network need the same protections as any computer connected to the Internet. Install antivirus and anti-spyware software, and keep them up to date. If your firewall was shipped in the "off" mode, turn it on.

3) Turn off identifier broadcasting. Most wireless routers have a mechanism called identifier broadcasting. It sends out a signal to any device in the vicinity announcing its presence. You don't need to broadcast this information if the person using the network already knows it is there. Hackers can use identifier broadcasting to home in on vulnerable wireless networks. Note the SSID name so you can connect manually. Disable the identifier broadcasting mechanism if your wireless router allows it.

4) Change the identifier on your router from the default. The identifier for your router is likely to be a standard default ID assigned by the manufacturer to all hardware of that model. Even if your router is not broadcasting its identifier to the world, hackers know the default IDs and can use them to try to access your network. Change your identifier to something only you know, and remember to configure the same unique ID into your wireless router and your computer so they can communicate. Use a password that's at least ten characters long—the longer your password, the harder it is for hackers to break. (See the next section on passwords for more advice here.)

5) Change your router's preset password for administration. The manufacturer of your wireless router probably assigned it a standard default password that allows you to set up and operate the router. Hackers know these default passwords, so change it to something only you know. The longer the password, the tougher it is to crack.

6) Allow only specific computers to access your wireless network. Every computer that is able to communicate with a network is assigned its own unique Media Access Control (MAC) address. Wireless routers usually have a mechanism to allow only devices with particular MAC addresses

access to the network. Some hackers have mimicked MAC addresses, so don't rely on this step alone.

7) Turn off your wireless network when you know you won't use it. Hackers cannot access a wireless router when it is shut down. If you turn the router off when you're not using it, you limit the amount of time that it is susceptible to a hack.

8) Don't assume that public "hot spots" are secure. Many cafés, hotels, airports, and other public establishments offer wireless networks for their customers' use. These "hot spots" are convenient, but they may not be secure. Ask the proprietor what security measures are in place.

9) Be careful about the information you access or send from a public wireless network. To be on the safe side, you may want to assume that other people can access any information you see or send over a public wireless network. Unless you can verify that a hot spot has effective security measures in place, it may be best to avoid sending or receiving sensitive information over that network.

Passwords

The average person has in excess of over ten passwords. Managing all of these passwords can be a daunting task for everyone. In order to facilitate the use of all of our passwords, we usually pick passwords that are simple for us to remember. This is where the problem begins. If someone wants to figure out your password, one of the most common schemes for doing so is dictionary software. A sophisticated online thief can use a dictionary program and check every word in the dictionary in less than three minutes.

When selecting passwords, try not to use common words, family names, family members' dates of birth, your mother's maiden name, your pet's name, or any word that can be figured out easily by the online thieves.

Some other solutions to selecting passwords are as follows:

- Misspell a word. This may protect you from a dictionary attack.
- Consider using the mnemonic method of memorization: instead of using the word "soccer" as a password change it to "ILTPSOS" for: I like to play soccer on Sunday.
- Use a combination of upper and lower case letters, including numbers such as: Ad3NGg36c.

Keeping track of all the various passwords can be difficult, especially since we need to change these on a regular basis for security purposes. Some will recommend keeping a record on your computer and others will say a paper version is best. Whichever method you choose to record your passwords, make sure only you know where they are and don't tell anyone what they are unless you need them to access your accounts or other personal access points. *Never* enter your passwords on a computer that is not in your control. This would include public computers at the library or in Internet cafés. *Never* record your passwords or personal identification numbers (PINs) on any of your debit cards or beside your computer. If you think your personal information has been compromised, do not hesitate to change all your passwords. Safe management of your passwords and PINs will assist in eliminating the opportunities for fraudsters to access your computer data, personal accounts, and other assets.

Online Security

Whether you use a Windows-based PC, a Mac, or a computer running Linux, you are still vulnerable to virus attacks. All three have experienced increases in attacks over the past few years. There was a time when only the Windows-based PCs were being attacked, but the identity thieves and scam artists are going after everyone now. According to the FBI, the likelihood of a business's local area network (LAN) being attacked by a virus or spyware is significantly high, as on-line thieves are constantly developing ways to hack into as many computers as they can.

To the hackers, it's a game or a conquest, and to some, it's a business where they seek your personal information for their financial gain. As soon as you modify your firewall, an-tivirus, and anti-spyware, the hackers find new ways to gain access to your private information. It is important to follow some well-established rules to improve your online security, such as not answering phishing scams, not opening suspi-cious attachments, and avoiding file sharing. If you want to avoid becoming a victim of online identity theft, you should keep up to date on new software and hardware in addition to modifying your online activity.

Spyware
Hackers are constantly trying to access your computer to collect your personal information without your knowledge or consent. The software used to perform this invasive act is called spyware and its use is growing exponentially world-wide. Spyware can look at many of your activities, such as In-ternet sites you visit, or access personal information, such as passwords and usernames. In the wrong hands, this informa-tion can cause many problems for you if it is sold to a third party who uses your personal information to gain access to your bank accounts or if someone steals your identity.

Many spyware software programs also deliver those nasty pop-up ads that we all dislike. Some of these pop-up ads can be very inappropriate for young children. In some cases the software will run various processes that will slow your computer down while you are trying to use it.

Spyware is often automatically downloaded from websites you visit or it can enter unannounced when you download another program. You should always read the user agreements for software that you download as the fine print may mention some form of spyware you will inadvertently agree to host.

Spyware is also known as snoopware, PC surveillance, key logger, system recorders, parental control software, PC recorder, detective software, Internet monitoring software, and Trojan horse programs. It can enter your computer hidden within software you wanted. Some people unknowingly load software to assist with spyware. Those cute little animated icons from www.hotbar.com have a privacy statement and it says quite plainly: "Hotbar collects and stores information about the web pages you view and the data you enter in search engine search fields while using the software."[13]

Spyware Story

Cynthia, a hairdresser from Vancouver, got her first computer three years ago, and she enjoyed receiving e-mails from her old high-school friends. She also liked to look at the latest beauty products online, although she never purchased any. She was a single mother supporting two sons, and the primary use of the computer was for the boys to look up information for school projects.

However, over the last year, Cynthia noticed her computer seemed to be processing more slowly. In fact, she and her two boys had stopped using the computer altogether because it was so slow that it was unusable.

Over Christmas, she wanted to purchase some small gifts for some of the people she worked with. In particular, she wanted to locate some live ladybugs to give to one of the girls at work. So, not having a computer to use at home, she borrowed her grandmother's computer to locate and purchase the ladybugs. After a short time, she noticed her grandmother's computer seemed to be moving slowly too, so she decided that computers were just not for her.

Cynthia's new boyfriend, however, was a computer science student, and when she told him about the slow computers, he guessed the problem right away: spyware. He downloaded a spyware detection program and confirmed his diagnosis. It took him several days to untangle the mess, but eventually the spyware was removed and the computers were back to normal. He installed up-to-date antivirus and security software for Cynthia and her grandmother, and they were soon both back online. However, the story does not end here.

While Cynthia was using her grandmother's computer, she had received a pop-up ad announcing she had won a $500 prize. All she had to do was answer a few questions and she could claim her $500 shopping spree to a local department store. Cynthia answered the questions, and then was told she had to buy two small items before getting her gift certificate. She ordered the two least expensive items from the gift menu, gave her credit card information as requested, and then attempted to put in the rest of the information to claim her $500 gift certificate.

The website, however, would not accept her information, and after several attempts, she gave up and decided to e-mail the site owners, hoping they would help her get things sorted out. She wrote to them twice but never received a reply. Her credit card was charged for the two "small items" she agreed to purchase but she never saw the $500 gift certificate.[14]

The clues that spyware is on a computer include[15]:

- a barrage of pop-up ads;
- a hijacked browser—a browser that takes you to sites other than those you type into the address box;
- a sudden or repeated change in your computer's Internet home page;
- new and unexpected toolbars;

- new and unexpected icons on the system tray at the bottom of your computer screen;
- keys that don't work (for example, the "tab" key that might not work when you try to move to the next field in a web form);
- random error messages; and/or
- sluggish or very slow performance when saving files or opening programs.

Spyware can also be associated with software that displays advertisements, which is called adware, or software that tracks personal information, but that does not mean all software that provides ads or tracks your online activities is bad. If you sign up for a free music service, you "pay" for the service by agreeing to receive targeted ads. By understanding the terms and agreeing to them, you may have decided that it is a fair tradeoff.

To protect your computer from spyware or to at least limit it as much as possible, you need to install up-to-date anti-spyware. Anti-spyware helps protect your computer against pop-ups, slow performance, and security threats caused by spyware and other unwanted software. To keep up with the latest forms of spyware, you must keep your anti-spyware updated.

According to Microsoft, many kinds of unwanted software, including spyware, are designed to be difficult to remove. If you try to uninstall this software like any other program, you might find that the program reappears as soon as you restart your computer. For PC users, Windows Defender is a free program designed to protect you against spyware. You can configure Windows Defender to update automatically. It also features real-time protection, a monitoring system that recommends actions against spyware when it's detected and minimizes interruptions.

Spyware Protection and Avoidance Tips
- Run a spyware detection and removal program.
- Avoid clicking anywhere unless you know it's safe. Before spyware can be installed on your computer, you usually have to click on something.
- Avoid clicking on pop-up ads. Sometimes creators of deceptive software use pop-up ads and dialogs to trick people into loading their software. Instead, try to close the web page or dialog by clicking the "X" in the top right corner of the window or by closing your browser, then reopening it.
- Don't install or download anything without knowing exactly what it is. Your computer can become the target of spyware when you download Internet data such as utilities, games, toolbars, media players, or other software. Be cautious; carefully read all agreements and privacy statements. Some will actually tell you that if you install the program, you will install some spyware with the software.
- Learn to use the options in your browser that allow you to clear the cache, cookies, and offline files.
- Keep your web browser security setting at medium or higher.
- Always keep current with operating system security updates.
- Install a personal firewall to stop uninvited users from accessing your computer. A firewall blocks unauthorized access to your computer and will alert you if spyware already on your computer is sending information out.

Firewalls
A firewall is a software program or piece of hardware that helps screen out hackers, viruses, and worms that try to reach your computer over the Internet. A firewall is essential, but you also need antivirus and anti-spyware software. If you use

a computer at home, the most effective and important first step you can take to help protect your computer is to turn on a firewall. If you don't have a firewall, get one set up today! Using a computer without a firewall is like going on vacation and leaving the front door to your home and all the windows wide open. A firewall creates a protective barrier between your computer and the Internet. This makes your connection invisible to Internet hackers. A firewall keeps others from seeing your confidential information. It helps prevent others from being able to access your computer and retrieve personal information such as banking information or passwords.

If you have more than one computer connected in the home, or if you have a small-office network, it is important to protect every computer. You should have a hardware firewall (such as a router) to protect your network, but you should also use a software firewall on each computer to help prevent the spread of a virus in your network if one of the computers becomes infected.

If your computer is part of a business, school, or other organizational network, you should follow the policy established by the network administrator. In some cases, network administrators may configure all computers on the network so that you cannot turn the firewall on while your computer is connected to the network. In those cases, you should ask your network administrator for guidance on whether you need a firewall on your computer.

How to Choose a Firewall

There are three basic types of firewalls available to choose from:

- Software firewalls.
- Hardware routers.
- Wireless routers.

In order to determine which type of firewall is best for you, you should understand what your needs are: How many computers will use a firewall? What operating system do you use? (Microsoft Windows, Mac OS, or Linux.) Once you have identified your needs, there are several options, each with its own pros and cons.

Software Firewalls

If you own a single computer, it is probably best to choose a software firewall. The good thing about software firewalls is they are available from many software companies and they don't require any computer wiring or additional hardware.

Hardware Routers

If you have a home network (or office network) the hardware router is a good choice since you can connect multiple computers and they will have the same firewall protection. The only downside is that hardware routers require wiring, which could cause clutter in your computer area.

Wireless Routers

Wireless routers are great for connecting many computers in a network and they can offer built-in firewall connections for computers that connect through the Wi-Fi broadcast signal. This form of connection is great for laptops as well as desktop computers since it offers multiple connections with no wires.

You may have to purchase a hardware firewall because not all wireless routers have one built in. The major area of concern with wireless Internet is the security of the broadcast signal. If someone has the right equipment, they can intercept your signals, so you need to be cautious when setting up your wireless router. As we mentioned earlier, you need to follow a set plan to eliminate the chance of strangers accessing your Internet signal.

If you don't use a firewall, you should start using one today to make your Internet experience safe and protect the personal information stored on your computer. The dangers of connecting to the Internet are growing everyday and the firewall is just one piece of protection. You also need to install and continuously update your anti-spyware and antivirus software as well as any other software updates that provide any form of online security.

Antivirus Software

Antivirus software is a computer program that must be on every computer you own or use. The program is designed to detect, prevent, and take action to disarm or remove malicious software programs such as viruses and worms. A virus is not a good thing to have on your computer as it could cause major problems for you and all computers connected to your network. The virus could also send itself to all those listed in your e-mail address book and completely destroy all of your friends', work associates' and family's computers by causing them to crash when the virus does its nasty work. In addition, viruses are designed to corrupt or delete data as well as interfere with a computer's operation. In order to prevent current viruses from infecting your computer, you should update your antivirus software regularly or set up the software to automatically update when there are changes to the software.

Nothing can guarantee the security of your computer 100%; however, staying current with this software can reduce the chances of a virus attacking your computer. Since no security method is guaranteed, it's important to backup critical files on a regular basis before you encounter a virus or other problems.

Steps to Help Avoid Viruses
1) Use an Internet firewall.
2) Subscribe to industry standard antivirus software, and

keep it up to date.

3) Never open an e-mail attachment from someone you don't know.

4) Avoid opening an e-mail attachment from someone you know, unless you know exactly what the attachment is. The person sending you the attachment may be unaware that it contains a virus.

5) Delete chain e-mails and junk e-mail. Do not open, forward, or reply to them.

6) Do not download any files from strangers.

In some cases, when you install a new software program, you may need to turn off your antivirus software during the installation process. Be sure to turn it back on again when the installation has completed.

Here are a few indicators that your computer might be infected by a virus[16]:

- Your computer stops responding or locks up often.
- Your computer runs more slowly than normal.
- Your computer restarts on its own and then fails to run normally.
- Your computer crashes and restarts every few minutes.
- Applications on your computer are not working correctly.
- Disk drives or disks are not accessible.
- You are constantly having trouble printing.
- You see dialogue boxes and distorted menus.
- You see unusual error messages.

In some instances, these indicators could also be hardware or software problems that have nothing to do with a virus. Unless you run and install up-to-date antivirus software on your computer, there is no way to be certain whether your computer is infected with a virus. It is extremely important that you install and run an antivirus software program as soon as possible.

Protect You and Your Computer

- Install anti-spyware.
- Install antivirus software.
- Apply updates frequently or automatically.
- Install software firewall.
- Install a basic hardware firewall between the Internet and your computer.
- Use strong password protocols.
- Change your passwords regularly and use hard-to-guess passwords.
- Don't give out your password—ever!
- Back up critical files often and in a couple of ways.
- Buy a surge-protected power bar for your computer.
- Permanently destroy all deleted files, don't trust the re- cycle bin or trash.
- Sanitize your hard drive before giving, selling, or dis- posing of your computer.
- Protect your privacy by cleaning up all tracks of your In- ternet and computer activities.
- Be sure to set up your operating system and web browser software properly, and update them regularly.
- Filter or block unsolicited e-mails.
- Consider encrypting your e-mail.
- Never install a wireless networking device unless you have discussed the risks with a security consultant.
- Be skeptical of things on the Internet.
- Know whom you're dealing with.
- Online offers that look too good to be true usually are.
- Clear the cache of your browser after visiting secure sites.
- Use care when downloading files from the Internet, read- ing e-mail with attachments, and installing programs.
- Find out whom to contact if something goes wrong on- line.

Additional tips for online banking:

- Ensure the "memorize passwords function" or "auto-complete" is disabled when conducting online banking.
- Never walk away from your computer without properly signing out from online banking.
- Review monthly financial statements promptly and report any discrepancies to your bank immediately.
- Never use a public computer (in a library or coffee shop) to do banking or personal and confidential transactions on the Internet.

Chapter 5

Mortgage and Title Fraud

Maria was happily married to Joe for over twenty years. They owned a beautiful home in Toronto and had two teenage daughters. Last year, Maria decided to take her two daughters to Italy to spend some time with her family and help her daughters get a better understanding of their cultural heritage.

They flew off to Milan and had a marvelous time for two months. They flew back to Toronto on a Monday and caught a cab to their home, since Joe couldn't be reached by phone. They pulled into the driveway of their home and noticed that a car they didn't recognize was in the driveway. They assumed Joe was home and had some company over.

Maria and the girls unloaded their bags and went to the front door. It was locked, so Maria pulled out her key and put it into the lock and tried to turn it. The key didn't work in the lock and they couldn't open the door. They could see lights on inside the house and assumed Joe must have been home, so she knocked on the door.

A boy of about twelve opened the door and said, "Hello."

Maria stepped into the house and said, "Who are you and where is Joe?" A man stepped up behind the boy and said,

"Hello, may I help you?"

Maria was getting a little confused.

"Is Joe here?" she asked.

"I don't know any Joe. Who are you and what do you want?" he replied.

"I am Maria and this is my house. What are you doing here?"

"Excuse me, this is our house. We just moved in two weeks ago, and we did buy the house from Joe, is that who you are referring to?"

"This is my house and we didn't sell it. I have been in Italy for two months with my two daughters, what is happening here?"

What happened in this story is classic title and mortgage fraud. While Maria was away, her husband, Joe, and his girlfriend of some eight years sold the house and disappeared. The girlfriend had impersonated Maria with the realtor and the lawyer and she and Joe had sold the house to an innocent unsuspecting buyer. What happens to the innocent purchaser and what happens to innocent Maria? What happens to the lender who has a mortgage on a property with the ownership in question? What happens to the lawyer, realtor, and mortgage broker who were all duped by Joe and his accomplice?

This is what this chapter is all about. We will be looking at how mortgage and title fraud happens, what the consequences for the innocent owners and purchasers are, and what remedies are available to recover your home and your money. We will also review, in some detail, how to prevent becoming a victim of mortgage and title fraud in Canada.

What Is Mortgage and Title Fraud?

Mortgage fraud is really any approach with the intent of obtaining a mortgage under false pretenses. Mortgage fraud is a theft of all or a portion of the mortgage proceeds. There is a variety of schemes used, but it can be as simple as falsifying income on a loan application or as sophisticated as defrauding a financial institution by obtaining a mortgage using fraudulent ID and impersonating the property's true owner.

For example, say you own your own home free and clear with no mortgage and a fraud artist obtains information about you and prepares false ID. The fraudster then goes to a mortgage broker impersonating you and obtains a mortgage on your home. The fraudster gets the money and you don't discover anything about the mortgage until the lender calls to inform you that your mortgage payments are in arrears and they are about to foreclose on your home unless you bring the mortgage up to date immediately. It's that simple.

Title fraud occurs when the fraud artists obtains detailed information about you and your property and, with a forged ID, changes the ownership of your home into their name or a fictional name. Your house now belongs to the fraud artist without your knowledge. Again, it's that simple and it's happening throughout Canada more and more every day.

Mortgage and title fraud is thought to be the fastest growing type of fraud in Canada. The *Calgary Herald* reported in March 2006 that "mortgage fraud hits $1.5 billion a year. Easy to do, often lucrative, real estate agents say it is growing quickly across Canada."[17] Since 2000, The *Toronto Star,* in particular, has been focusing many articles discussing mortgage fraud.

Many newspapers across Canada have featured articles highlighting the increasing occurrences of mortgage and title fraud. In the United States, mortgage fraud has been a concern for a number of years and has been growing rapidly since the early '90s. Even the FBI has become interested in this growing type of fraud, feeling that it may have a detrimental effect on the entire U.S. economy. Due to the recent increases in fraud and the dollar values, Toronto Police Services has established a mortgage fraud investigation group.

There is big money available in the mortgage fraud business and the penalties have been minor at best. Organized crime has also discovered the easy money available through mortgage and title fraud. The average fraud could net the fraudster $200,000 to $400,000 or more with less than a full week's work.

Mortgage fraud usually involves several people and is a challenge to investigate because the perpetrators use false identification and are often difficult to track down. When money is this easy to obtain, you can be assured more of the criminal element in Canada will get involved and it is your home they are looking at as a potential target. The risk of jail time is not strong in Canada. For example, there was a recent case of one convicted mortgage fraudster who was sentenced to thirty days in jail to be served on weekends. Another fraudster convicted of thirty-three charges of fraud was sentenced to thirty-eight months. Not much of a deterrent considering the large sums of money involved. We expect mortgage fraud to continue to grow in every province across Canada.

How Easy Is It to Steal Your Home?

The real estate and lending activities in Canada involve a number of participants who might collude to perpetrate a fraud. So many different people and professions are involved in a real estate transaction that it is difficult to detect and prevent fraud before it happens, and it is equally difficult to investigate after the fact.

A lender rarely knows a mortgage is fraudulent until it goes into default and the mortgage payments are several months overdue. Several other factors increase the risk of fraud, including the land transfer system itself, the rather impersonal nature of mortgage lending where many mortgage brokers may never see their client, and the competitiveness of the industry. The ease of access to credit information and technology enables fraudsters to forge and counterfeit documents as well as enable lenders to automate many aspects in the loan approval process. It would appear that whatever safeguards are implemented for mortgage fraud, the professional fraudster finds a way around them.

Greed is the main motivator for fraud artists—big money with minimal risk and effort. The opportunities are due to the inherent weaknesses in the system and fraudsters exploit these weaknesses. The electronic land registration in Ontario provides information regarding the property, such as legal description, registered owners, and any mortgages registered against the property. This system is owned and operated by Teranet, Inc. Your mortgage and title is public record and anyone can go to the registry office and look up the information on your home.

In Ontario, all a fraudster requires is an understanding of the conveyance system as well as a specifically encrypted diskette and access to the system. Real estate lawyers, their staff and financial institutions, as well as real estate agents, appraisers, and surveyors have this access. Anyone can apply to Teranet as long as they meet their security screening and pay the access fees. Once approved, Teranet provides the diskette to access the system. The fraudsters can access Teranet legitimately or by merely using someone else's diskette and pass phrase. A property can be transferred without any face-to-face interaction at the land registry office. The registration of your home can be switched to another person quite simply through fraudulent means and all for under $100.

The Devil You Know

Many fraud situations occur when a family member is involved in the fraudulent activity. Maria lost her home through fraud because her husband and his girlfriend sold their jointly registered home without her written consent. The consent was fraudulent. These situations are extremely difficult to identify prior to the sale or prior to advancing the mortgage.

A headline in the *Toronto Star* published November 18,

2006, states, "Sister's signature forged in sale." When Sharon Dunford's mother died in June 2000, she had willed the family home to Dunford and her sister equally. Dunford's sister was allowed to live in the family home for as long as she wanted, but the taxes, utilities, and upkeep were her responsibility. Dunford dropped by the house in July 2006 and was informed by a neighbour that the house had been sold. As Dunford was still half owner, she was obviously surprised by this event as she had not signed any documentation to sell the house nor had any intention of selling.

The sale was closed at the lawyer's office with someone posing as Sharon Dunford. Dunford's signature had been forged and the jointly owned house was sold to an unsuspecting third party. What happened is that Dunford lost the ownership of her home and an innocent buyer now owns it through fraudulent means. This is now a case for the police, the lawyers, and the courts.

Another recent case involved a spouse with a gambling problem. As the debts mounted there was only one way out: negotiating a mortgage on the family home through a broker. The spouse forged the husband's signature and the mortgage funds were advanced to pay off the gambling debts. Needless to say, the gambling problem persisted and the mortgage went in arrears. The husband eventually discovered his wife had mortgaged their home without his consent. This certainly made for interesting dinner conversations once the true situation came to light. The challenge lies in what happens next. In this case, the courts held that the fraudulent mortgage was valid as it was properly registered. The previously free and clear home now was encumbered without the spouse's consent. This is a difficult situation for the innocent spouse to be in.

Gambling, alcohol, and drug addictions contribute to the devil-you-know type of fraud but so does simple greed. A family member being involved in a fraud makes it difficult to detect. They already know all the details about the individual and one of them is legitimate. Although detection is nearly impossible, it is easy to discover after the fact, but by then it is too late for everyone involved. The money has been paid out and it is usually then that the fraud investigation begins. All parties in the transactions are questioned on the procedures that allowed this to happen. It is very time consuming and costly for the brokers, lawyers, lenders, realtors, and the innocent victim as well.

Power of Attorney Fraud

A couple owns a condo unit, which is rented out for investment purposes. While they are out of the country, their son forges a power of attorney that purports to give him authority to deal with the property. Using the forged documents, he goes to a mortgage broker and places a mortgage on the condo to finance his personal business that is in some financial difficulty. The parents return home and discover the mortgage when their tenant receives a notice from the lender, asking them to pay future rents to the lender. These family situations are extremely painful, personal, and costly to resolve.

The Devil You Don't Know

In this case, a stranger manages to obtain information about you and steals your identity. With this information they are well prepared to steal your house and sell it or simply put a mortgage on your property without your knowledge and make off with your money.

There are several types of approaches used.

Tenant Fraud

The *Toronto Star* reported in an article published August 26, 2006, "An eighty-nine-year-old man had been left both heartbroken and betrayed after his North York bungalow was stolen from him in the rising wave of title fraud."[18]

Paul Reviczky fled communist Hungary in 1957 and came to Canada. In 1980, he purchased a rental property to provide income for his relatives' education in Hungary. He lived alone, only a few kilometers from his rental property.

In June 2006, a neighbour who happened to be a real estate agent told him that she had noticed that he had sold his rental property in May. Reviczky said she must be mistaken as he still had his rental property and had no intention of ever selling the property. The neighbour then went home and verified on the MLS system that his rental property had been sold.

Apparently, an Aaron Paul Reviczky had purported to be Paul's grandson and provided a forged power of attorney that gave him the legal authority to sell the house. Reviczky has no grandson named Aaron; actually, he has no grandson at all.

The police later believed the tenant of the rental property forged his name on the power of attorney and sold the house on his behalf for $450,000 to legitimate purchasers who took out a mortgage for $337,500.

When Reviczky contacted his lawyer, he was told that he might lose his house, even though he was an innocent victim of fraud. At that time, Ontario law recognized the transaction as valid if properly registered. He was informed that he would receive some financial compensation from the Land Assurance Fund, but that could take several years and would entail legal fees at his expense.

Reviczky wants his property back, not the compensation. The new owners want to keep their house. We have two innocent parties both facing significant personal turmoil and uncertainty of unravelling the situation.

Both the tenant and the money are long gone. All seemed just fine for the new purchasers. They met the supposed owner and openly met at the house. There was no reason to doubt the validity of the transaction at that stage.

Tenant frauds are difficult to identify for the unsuspecting purchasers, realtors, and lawyers. The key in this transaction was the power of attorney and the need to verify its validity. A call to Paul Reviczky would have revealed the fraud immediately, but no call was made and both the original owner and the new owner must deal with the aftermath.

The lawyer involved has refused to discuss the case and had witnessed the power of attorney. The purchasers' lawyer feels the new purchasers are the innocent victims and have suffered financially and emotionally through no fault of their own. They did nothing wrong yet had to continue to pay their mortgage payments and could not occupy the home they had purchased. Their ownership was now being questioned.

Reviczky cannot enter the house either; he no longer holds title to the property. The house sits empty and is quickly falling into disrepair. No one cuts the grass or cleans up garbage while lawyers negotiate with each other to decide the fate of the house and the innocent owner and purchaser.

Perhaps a clue in this case involves the rental situation. In March of that year, Reviczky put a For Rent sign on the front lawn of his property. The previous tenants had been with him for twelve years and had relocated. Within a few days, he rented the property to new tenants who paid $2,500 in cash for first and last months' rent. The house remained empty and they paid the next month's rent in cash as well. As a landlord, it might have been prudent to question why a tenant pays cash and why they would delay moving in.

Mortgage by an Imposter

A fraudster posing as the owner of your home arranges a $450,000 mortgage to be placed on the mortgage-free property. The loan was structured so that no payments were due for six months. An interest reserve was taken by the lender, which meant that just under $400,000 was actually advanced, while the balance was held back to make payments during the six-month reserve period. When the interest reserve ran out, the loan went into default and the fraud was discovered when the lender made demand on the loan to the true owner of the property. Think of how you would feel if a lender informed you of a $450,000 mortgage on your home and demands payment. It happens, and it is happening more often.

The Susan Lawrence Story

Perhaps the most publicized fraud story in recent years involved Susan Lawrence. The story helped raise public awareness of this growing crime in Canada. Lawrence, a 55 year-old widow, had her house stolen out from under her by identity thieves who also left her with a $300,000 mortgage in default.

A press release from First Canadian Title quotes Lawrence, "I never imagined that putting a For Sale sign on my front lawn would result in being defrauded out of my home [...] I can't stress enough how devastating, financially and emotionally—to have to fight to get my home back over the past twelve months."

After a year-long struggle that involved getting back the title of her home and going all the way to the Ontario Court of Appeals to get the fraudulent mortgage registered on her home dismissed, Lawrence is once again the rightful owner of her home and the fraudulent mortgage has been discharged.

The fraudsters targeted the home because it was for sale and they forged her signature to sell her century-old North York home to accomplices, who then took out a mortgage to pay for it. When the accomplices defaulted on the loan, the lender foreclosed on the property. Lawrence was left with only two choices: lose her home or pay off the debt.

At that time, an Ontario court ruling in a similar case the previous year had interpreted the Ontario Land Titles Act to mean homeowners were held accountable once the title change had been registered under the provincial land title system, even if done so fraudulently.

Susan Lawrence decided to fight back and hired Toronto lawyer Morris Cooper to appeal the previous ruling in what's known as the "Household Realty" case.

After a year of legal wrangling, the Ontario Court of Appeal ruled in Lawrence's favour and also ordered the mortgage lenders to pay $25,000 toward her legal costs.

Lawrence is now telling her story across Canada and warning all homeowners of the dangers of mortgage fraud and the tremendous personal anguish one must go through to regain ownership of your own home. Susan Lawrence's story is a perfect example of how—despite existing checks and balances in the system—crooks are able to exploit weaknesses in the system and can steal the ownership of your home and mortgage that same property.

The Fictitious Law Firm

Fraudsters can be quite creative in finding ways to defraud banks of hundreds of thousands of dollars. One fraudster created a fictitious law firm, using the names of real lawyers to add credibility to their scheme. First Canadian Title investigated this fraud, which involved fake ID, fake appraisals, bogus listing agreements, fake agreements of purchase and sale, as well as phony employment verifications. The lender in question was provided with a "report" from the law firm including what appeared to be registered transfers and mortgages. In fact, the properties in question were never transferred and the mortgages were never registered. In this case, only the lender was the innocent victim because the entire purchase, sale, and mortgages were all fabrications.

Fraud across Canada

The *Calgary Herald* reported on March 18, 2006 a fraud case in British Columbia. A private mortgage lender using his own money arranged a $250,000 mortgage for an elderly BC man against a $500,000 house. The man claimed he was planning to sell and wanted a good mortgage on the property to enhance the sale price so a prospective buyer could simply transfer the mortgage upon purchase. A lawyer was engaged and verified the man's identification. A mortgage broker arranged the financing through the private lender.

It wasn't until after funds were advanced that the lender discovered that the man in question didn't own the house and had fooled everyone involved in the transaction. When the realtor who was supposedly listing the property was informed that the private lender had a mortgage on it, the realtor said that it was impossible. There can't be a mortgage on the property because the registered owner is deceased.

You can imagine how everyone felt after being duped in this transaction, and now comes the inevitable legal wrangling to try and unravel the transaction and the lender's predicament of holding a fraudulent mortgage on a property that was fraudulently arranged. Fortunately for this lender, he had the expertise to arrange title insurance on the transaction. The title company paid off the mortgage under its fraud coverage.

The *Calgary Herald* reported that after a six-month investigation, the commercial crime unit in conjunction with the Alberta Government Services charged Lloyd Lewis Mason of Calgary with one count of fraud and one count of fraud in relation to making a false registration of title. The case involved the unlawful transfer of a title to another person without the knowledge of the true owner. That person then took out an $110,000 mortgage on the property. The fraud came to light when the true owner attempted to pay property taxes and the City of Calgary notified the owner that he no longer owned the property.

Put yourself in these innocent owners' shoes for a moment. You discover you no longer own your home from the city's property tax department. What is your first reaction? Disbelief, anger, frustration, and finally fear? Wondering what to do next is always the question, and each province is different.

There was no title insurance protection on this transaction, so it had to be handled by a lawyer to regain title to the home and deal with the fraudulent mortgage on the home as well. These are frightening times for innocent homeowners targeted by fraud artists.

In 2005, six residents in Edmonton, Alberta, were charged in the largest mortgage fraud case in the province's history. A total of 118 properties in Edmonton and 6 in Camrose were fraudulently mortgaged for a total of over $30 million. The Real Estate Council of Alberta measured the occurrences of mortgage fraud in a twelve-month period and identified 2,750 occurrences. They used a conservative assessment on the mortgage value of $100,000 per fraud and arrived at an astonishing $275 million in fraudulent mortgages in Alberta alone. This is indeed a growing crime in Canada and is a concern for all homeowners and those involved in the mortgage and real estate business.

The Wirick Case in BC

The Law Society of British Columbia in its Benchers' Bulletin of November/December 2005 provided an update from the Special Compensation Fund Committee on the Wirick case. The Law Society of British Columbia, after four years of investigation, recently approved $32.5 million in payments to cover a multi-million-dollar real estate fraud case involving lawyer Martin Wirick. This high-profile case involved transactions between 1998 and 2002 and affected hundreds of victims in the scheme. As a result of this case, BC lawyers contribute to a special compensation fund to reimburse members of the public for losses associated with fraud and lawyer-related issues.

Mr. Wirick had acted for a Vancouver real estate developer and for certain nominees in the sale of various properties. He admitted that he had misappropriated trust funds in real estate transactions by failing to pay out and discharge mortgages, and had instead applied the funds to other purposes, in breach of his undertakings. As of December 2005, the Special Compensation Fund Committee had considered 495 claims of the 555 total claims. Of these, 347 have been decided and $32.5 million have been approved for payment. Fifty-one claims have been withdrawn and another 150 claims have been adjourned for further investigation. The total amount originally claimed against Mr. Wirick amounted to almost $80 million.

Innocent purchasers of these properties never had the original mortgage discharged, and when they purchased the property, they arranged their own mortgage. At the end of the day, the innocent purchaser was left with the original mortgage of the previous owner and their own mortgage by their lender. The total mortgage amount was well in excess of the value since there were two mortgages on each property.

The innocent purchaser and lender then had to apply to the Special Compensation Fund for remedy and to attempt to cover their own legal expenses incurred over the four-year investigation period.

Oklahoma Fraud: Valuation Fraud

This type of valuation fraud has been around for a long time. It involves the purchase of a home and then flipping or reselling that home at an inflated value over the true value and gaining a larger mortgage than the property is worth. Often there is collusion between a broker and an unscrupulous appraiser, and often the purchaser is an accomplice as well. Recent changes to valuation models by mortgage insurance companies leave them open to valuation fraud by simply changing the postal code to a more affluent neighbourhood that substantially increases the market value of comparable houses.

Condo Parking Space Fraud

An interesting story of a condo fraud was published on the website of the Canadian Legal Information Institute (www.canlii.org). Between December 1998 and March 2002, fraudsters purchased various parking spaces and storage units in high-end condos for amounts ranging from $11,000 to $30,000. The fraudsters then presented these units as regular condo units and arranged mortgages on them for amounts approaching $200,000. The lawyer involved acted on all the transactions and failed to notice the many indications that these units were actually parking spaces or storage units and municipal assessment was well below the mortgage amount. The lender now has been forced to sell the spaces at significant loss and all the proceeds of almost $1.9 million have disappeared into the fraudsters' hands. The lawyer in question is awaiting the penalty hearing from the Law Society.

Red Flags of Potential Mortgage and Title Fraud

There are many indications during a fraudulent mortgage transaction that would give the suspicious lender, broker, or lawyer an opportunity to investigate the file further and actually halt the transaction before mortgage funds are advanced.

Lawyer Red Flags

The lawyer is the last defense against mortgage fraud since they see the fraudster face to face before the actual money changes hands. Identity theft is really at the core of most fraudulent activities, so confirming ID is a critical step in establishing a bona fide mortgage transaction.

* Check ID. Most lawyers in Canada now demand photo ID as a part of their closing procedures. However, photo ID is relatively easy to forge.

  In one case, a lawyer asked for ID from the woman arranging the mortgage. He looked at the ID and sensed something was wrong, so asked for her birthday that could be verified on the license. Without thinking, the woman reached for the ID to check what her birthday was. She immediately realized her error and jumped from the chair and rushed out of the office. One fraud stopped by an observant lawyer.

Some lawyers are using card readers to verify the driver's license magnetic stripe to ensure it is valid. This is a small price for a lawyer to pay to stay out of the newspapers by being duped by a fraud artist, not to mention the countless hours of investigations and reviews of files and business practices. These lawyers refer to their card readers as preventative medicine. Many lawyers use a magnifying glass on the ID to identify the small items imbedded into the print to foil potential fraudulent IDs. This simple method has actually halted fraudulent mortgages as soon as the ocular device was put onto the desk. Some fraudsters bolt when lawyers carefully inspect the ID. First Canadian Title has offered these ocular devices to law firms along with a tip sheet of what to look for to help identify forged IDs.

- Power of attorney. A transaction that includes a power of attorney should always be verified. Recent fraud cases in British Columbia have had power of attorneys signed in Asia or Europe and are difficult to verify. This should be a warning sign for further investigation.

- Sense of urgency. If the client, lender, or realtor is pressuring you (as a lawyer) to close this transaction immediately, you must question why they waited so long to move on this transaction. Why are they in such a rush now, at the last minute? This is a warning sign since most bona fide clients don't wait until a few days before closing to contact their lawyer.

- Know your client. If you don't know the referring source of the business and the property in question is not in your market area and neither is the current residence of the person obtaining the mortgage, a good question to ask is: "Why did you choose my office?" A simple rule of thumb for fraud is that if it looks to good to be true, it probably is. Does it make sense that this customer would deal with you?

- Cash back. Many lenders offer a cash back type of mortgage that offers anywhere from 1 to 8% of the mortgage amount in immediate cash to the customer on the closing date. Normally, this payment should be paid to the registered owner of the property. If the mortgage broker has the clients sign a letter of direction to pay the funds to a third party it is a red flag that should be investigated further. These cash backs can amount to anywhere from $10,000 to $20,000. If they go to a third party, the lawyer should ask why. If the cash back isn't going directly to the registered owner, something might be amiss.

- Follow the money. Refinances are an easy way to obtain funds fraudulently from someone else's mortgage-free home through identity theft. If a house is free and clear and the client wants a large mortgage or secured line of credit, this is worth investigating further and the lawyer should ask why. The funds on a refinance should never be paid to a third party. The funds should always be directed to the registered owner, which makes cashing the cheque more difficult. The fraudster must deal with a bank to cash the cheque and this is another opportunity to catch the fraud before the money is gone. Fraudsters will, of course, give any good reason and some not-so-good reasons to convince the lawyer that the proceeds should be paid elsewhere. Don't do it!

- Interest reserve. Fraudsters often prepare a good story about the need to have an interest reserve to pay for mortgage payments for the first six months or so. They may be borrowing the money for a new business and want to provide six months' breathing room to establish the company. Interest reserves are suspect and need further investigation. Fraudsters use interest reserves to allow a specific time frame before anyone discovers anything is wrong. The interest reserve period may be for three months or six months, or even a year in some cases, leaving them ample time to escape unnoticed and cover their trail. Eight months to a year later, when the fraud starts to get investigated, no one will remember the people or the transaction. The lawyer will wish he or she had looked a little closer at the interest reserve case when the police arrive to investigate.

Lawyer Checklists

Stephen Shub, a real estate lawyer in Toronto, has a personal and professional interest in title and mortgage fraud. He operates a law office that processes a substantial volume of residential real estate transactions. Shub knows that fraud artists target large and busy law firms in the belief that there could be gaps in their procedures. He has established his own procedures that have discovered fraud in action and has refused to close those suspicious files. He has a real estate checklist that must be completed on each and every file at his office. A suspicious response requires further investigation, and on several occasions, an outright refusal to complete the transaction. Please refer to the appendix for the checklist used by Stephen Shub's law office.

Many fraudsters will only provide a cell phone as the means to contact them because they don't want to provide the registered owner's home phone number. If a cell number is the only number provided, this is a red flag, especially if the client refuses to provide their home phone number. Any comments about this as being a surprise for their spouse or a request to take the documents home is another clear signal to ask more questions.

Lender Red Flags

Lenders are targeted with fraud because they are the providers of the funds. The lender has the opportunity to review the credit application and the credit check to ensure the validity of the transaction and the ability of the borrower(s) to repay. If the lender completes the application, they have the ability to check ID, but if completed by a mortgage broker, they expect the broker to verify ID.

Competition is fierce in the mortgage business and therefore susceptible to fraudsters. It is really important for all lenders and their mobile sales forces not to shortcut any steps in order to get the deal done.

- Brokers. A fraudster will almost always target a mortgage broker to complete the application and obtain the mortgage. Lenders in bank branches usually ask more questions than the fraudster would like so they avoid retail bank branches. Many brokers don't see their clients face to face, making the fraud easier. Banks processing mortgages through brokers are aware of the risks associated with these types of transactions and have implemented additional fraud and audit checks.

- Credit checks. The underwriting of a mortgage transaction is a key opportunity to verify information. When reviewing the credit bureau, the application should be matched to the information provided on the bureau and discrepancies vigorously investigated. Careful review of the employment letter often reveals small inaccuracies such as typos or homemade letterhead. Are there unexplained gaps in employment or residences? Did the client provide a cell phone number and no home telephone number? Conventional mortgages are not disclosed on the credit bureau as yet, so multiple mortgages and discharges are more difficult to identify. A large number of credit inquiries by other financial institutions is another red flag for the astute underwriter.

- ID checks. Lenders should always obtain verifiable photo ID from two sources.

- Appraisals. When in doubt, the lender, through the appraiser, should visit the house and talk to the owners. Verify that the appraisal does in fact represent current prices in the area. Appraisal fraud is common in Canada. The lender should choose the appraiser at all times. It would be quite embarrassing for a lender to discover a mortgage on a vacant lot that was booked originally on the basis of a house on that property.

Mortgage Broker Red Flags

As previously stated, fraudsters target mortgage brokers by design. Their acting as a roving sales force for lenders is the reason why fraudsters like them. They are available and they are eager to do business.

- Home free and clear. For a mortgage broker, the bigger the mortgage the more the commission, but you should always ask why someone who owns a home free and clear wants to borrow a large amount for the first time in years. Again, if the deal seems too good to be true, it may not be legitimate. The borrower may only want to borrow less than 80% of the home value so no high-ratio mortgage insurance is required or may want 50% of the home value as an equity takeout. These red flags should make the mortgage broker ask more questions.

- Referral. If a mortgage broker gets a referral from someone they don't know, this could be a red flag to investigate a little further. Why did they select you?

- ID. The mortgage application seems to have some gaps
and you only get a cell phone number. Employment letter is a photocopy and it's not a good one either. It's amaz-
ing what has been accepted as fake letters of employment,
including documents that have a misspelling of the
client's name. Check ID carefully and be aware of all the
little things that happen during the application process.

- Meet the client. With the advent of Internet applications,
an increasing number of mortgages are being approved
where no one has seen the customer. To avoid fraudulent
mortgage applications, it is suggested that mortgage brokers meet their client in their home. If it's legitimate, you
have a better chance to seal the deal and a better chance
to gain further referrals. If the mortgage request is fraudulent, they won't meet the broker at home and will try to
meet the broker somewhere else such as a coffee shop.

Realtor Fraud Red Flags
- Fraudsters only provide a cell phone number because
they don't want a landline linked to them or to the stolen
property. A renter committing fraud by selling the rental
property may provide a landline since he does in fact live
there.

- The vendor doesn't want a For Sale sign on the property
because this may attract attention from neighbours,
prompting them to ask questions or contact the real
owner.

- See if the client has a copy of the deed or old tax bill to verify property information. The fraudster will not have access to these documents.

- Always check photo ID of the registered owners of the property, but not just one of the registered owners but all owners on title. If it's a spousal fraud, one of the spouses will be unavailable to sign—this should serve as a warning sign.

- If the value stated by the vendor seems unrealistically high and they have a potential purchaser at that price, this could be valuation fraud.

- Review the red flags for the other professionals involved in the transaction.

- The deposit is paid directly to the vendor and not in trust.

Homeowner Red Flags
- When renting a property, be sure to do a complete investigation of the potential renter, including ID verification, credit bureau, employment verification, and bank check. You could also verify references from previous landlords.

- A renter paying cash in advance may indicate they don't want to use their bank account and may be setting you up to steal your home and sell it.

- Visit your rental property often in the first four months to assess what is happening and be suspicious of things that don't seem right.

- Retired people who vacation in the winter for an extended period of time are a prime target for fraudsters.

- Homes that are free and clear of any mortgages are targeted more often than mortgaged homes because the fraudsters won't have to spend time and energy discharging the existing mortgage. However, having a mortgage or a home equity line of credit on your home is no real protection against title and mortgage fraud.

In our research, almost everyone we talked to has indicated that before they discovered the fraud, they knew in the back of their mind that something didn't seem right. They ignored these warning signs and didn't investigate further and later found themselves involved in a fraudulent mortgage. The advice we received from numerous sources was: listen to your gut. Your experience and knowledge is a critical safeguard against fraud. The urgency of the matter or the opportunity to close a big deal might sway your instincts. Whether you are a realtor, lender, mortgage broker, lawyer, or consumer, you do have good instincts and should pay attention to them; they may save a potential fraud from being executed.

Consequences and Remedies

Several major companies including First Canadian Title, Stewart Title, Chicago Title, and TitlePLUS offer title insurance in Canada, and these four companies have the lion's share of the market.

Title insurance protects new and existing homeowners, as well as lenders, against losses as a result of title defects. It provides protection against issues such as real estate title fraud or forgery, unpaid liens, encroachment issues, construction liens, defects in title, and costs arising from building code violations.

For a one-time premium, a title insurance policy stays in effect for as long as the insured retains an interest in the property. Professor Emeritus Stanley W. Hamilton of the Sauder School of Business at the University of British Columbia, in his recent report, *Private Title Insurance: A Role within a Torrens System of Real Property Registration,* states: "Title insurance is now an important and valuable part of the conveyancing and mortgage lending scene in Canada."

In the situation of title fraud where there is a challenge to ownership, the title insurance company assumes responsibility for defending the homeowner's rights and/or the lender's rights, providing compensation when required. If the mortgage is unenforceable for the lender, the mortgage will be paid off by the insurer and discharged. This will bring both the lender and original homeowner back to the situation prior to the fraud. If the mortgage is enforceable against title, the insurer will pay the mortgage off on behalf of the owner if the owner has title insurance.

The no-fault claims resolution process includes managing the claim on behalf of the homeowner, defending their right of ownership, quickly paying off the invalid mortgage, covering any related costs associated with title rectification and retaining the assistance of a lawyer. Title companies understand how devastating and unimaginable an act such as title fraud can be to a homeowner. They also understand how frustrating and traumatic it is to be asked to defend what is rightfully yours. The experience of title insurers gained over the years in dealing with fraud will be a true support to those victimized by fraudsters.

The Law in Ontario

After all the media hype around consumers' growing concern over title and mortgage fraud, the Government of Ontario introduced Bill 152, which, among many other things, is intended to ensure that ownership of a property cannot be lost as a result of a fraudulent sale, counterfeit power of attorney, or the registration of a falsified mortgage. This bill was named the Ministry of Government Services Consumer Protection and Service Modernization Act, Bill 152. It amended the Land Registration Reform Act and the Land Titles Act since they do affect property owners.

Bill 152 speaks only to purported interest in land registered after October 19, 2006. Any fraudulent instruments registered prior to that date will not fall under this legislation but will be governed by the prior legislation and case law.

Under Bill 152, an innocent owner has the right to have their title restored if the ownership of the home has been transferred or sold fraudulently. A refinance mortgage registered fraudulently on an innocent owner's property, in most cases, will be void and the fraudulent mortgage discharged. In some cases of fraud, the government can ensure title is returned and compensation determined within ninety days.

The intent of the legislation is to protect innocent homeowners who fall victim to title or mortgage fraud. In most cases, no one will lose their home or have to pay a mortgage they didn't agree to. A fraudulent mortgage, even after registration, is void. The legislation includes measures to improve access to the Land Titles Assurance Fund as well as improving the response time of the fund. What this means remains to be seen as we have yet to see the results of this new legislation.

It is important for homeowners to know that there is still a process to follow in order to restore title and remove an invalid mortgage, and while title is being restored, the owner will be unable to sell or mortgage their property. This process will require the assistance of a lawyer and is, initially, at the homeowner's expense unless covered by title insurance.

This new legislation cannot stop real estate fraud. The money is easy, encouraging this type of fraud to continue. Many more innocent homeowners, lenders, and purchasers will become victims. Under Bill 152, an innocent purchaser of a home sold fraudulently will no longer own that house and the fund will hear the original owner's claim for compensation to pay off the fraudulent mortgage. In this instance, the mortgage is enforceable, but Bill 152 addresses the owner's rights to compensation and the lender will await the decision by the Assurance Fund. The new purchaser will have to apply to the fund for compensation to pay off the new mortgage. The lender will have no recourse to the fund in this instance and must rely on the new purchaser to apply and pay off the existing mortgage. The original homeowner gets title back, but a mortgage remains registered on the property until the Assurance Fund completes the claim filed by the new purchaser.

Both will be victims. The innocent original homeowner may be protected, but it is still unclear how this will occur: What will be required to prove innocence? How long will the process take? In the intervening time, no one really knows how it will play out or what costs will be involved in resolving the many issues. The innocent purchaser of a fraudulently sold home and the lender booking the mortgage will be required to apply to the Assurance Fund for compensation and this may have to be decided in court.

The Law in British Columbia

The BC government has tackled the problem of title and mortgage fraud in a different way. In this province, the ownership of a home sold fraudulently to an innocent purchaser will remain in the innocent purchasers name and the original owner must apply for financial recovery from the Assurance Fund.

The BC legislation only applies to ownership, so the lenders involved would have no claim against the property and must therefore apply to the Assurance Fund. In BC, the innocent purchaser must actually take possession of the home before rights of ownership are applied.

The interesting aspect here is that no matter how the law is enacted, there will always be an innocent victim, either the original homeowner or the new purchaser, not to mention the lender. The victim of the fraud must apply to the Assurance Fund for compensation.

The Law in Alberta, Saskatchewan, and Manitoba

The land titles system in Alberta, Saskatchewan and Manitoba is the Torrens System of land registration. This system has been in place since the late 1800s. It requires that the state maintain a register that contains a description of each parcel of land covered by the system, the name of the registered owner, and a description of the interest in the land claimed by persons other than the registered owners.

Ideally, the Torrens System embodies three fundamental principles:

- Indefeasibility and certainty of title;
- Compulsory registration of all transactions relating to land; and
- Compensation for any damages suffered as a result of the failure of the system.

In other words, once the certificate of title is registered and issued, it is guaranteed to be accurate. If a fraudster registers a mortgage fraudulently on your property, it is therefore considered to be valid and claims may be made to the Land Assurance Fund for compensation. If your home is sold under fraudulent conditions and the new registration and certificate of title is issued, it is also considered to be valid and is guaranteed to be accurate. Again, compensation from the Assurance Fund must be applied for. No easy solution to title and mortgage fraud really exists in any of the provinces in Canada. Most cases must end up in court to be decided, while the innocent foot the legal bill.

The Law in Atlantic Canada

Prince Edward Island and Newfoundland operate under the old registry system while Nova Scotia and New Brunswick have a new Land Title System.

In the Nova Scotia Land Title System, registered interests are protected but the system does not guarantee or protect recorded interests. Mortgages are considered to be recorded interests. If a title is stolen and conveyed to an unsuspecting purchaser and the ownership is recorded in the Land Registry System, that interest is protected by the system. The mortgage would be a recorded interest, which is not protected by the system, and the validity of the mortgage would be subject to litigation. The original owner could lose title to the home if fraudulently sold and registered, while the new owner is protected.

New Brunswick also has a Land Title System, where there is no distinction between registered and recorded interests, and they refer to these recorded interests as encumbrance holder. Therefore, New Brunswick, unlike Nova Scotia, guarantees all of the information noted in a certification of registered ownership. At this time, there has been no case to test this system on fraud. Typically, with no case law evident, the fraud would end up in court and the innocent homeowner would be liable for their own legal bills to regain title to their home and/or discharge the fraudulent mortgage.

Prince Edward Island and Newfoundland are the only two jurisdictions remaining with the traditional Land Registry System. Generally, a bona fide purchaser without knowledge of any fraud is protected under this system against unregistered documents. These systems are only notice systems and do not guarantee the validity of any documents recorded in the system. Therefore, if a mortgage was fraudulently entered into the system, the fraudulent mortgage or deed would be subject to litigation and determination by the court. Again, out of pocket legal expenses and worry for the innocent homeowner.

The Law in Quebec

Quebec operates under civil law, while the rest of Canada operates under common law. There have been very few fraudulent mortgage court cases in Quebec to establish precedent. The most famous real estate fraud case in Quebec involved former *La Presse* journalist François Trépanier, where fraudsters made away with $243,000 and forced Trépanier to endure considerable stress and legal costs to win back the title to his home in Montreal.

In Quebec, if a fraudulent transaction takes place and is registered, the innocent victim must pursue the notary who completed the transaction for the fraudster. This puts a huge responsibility on the notary involved in real estate as they become accountable for the legitimacy of the transaction and are open to being sued.

Quebec notaries have been checking IDs on a regular basis for about ten years now and are required to obtain two pieces of ID from each party to the transaction. With improved ID forgery techniques, this careful screening of clients may not be enough in Quebec to keep the professional fraudster at bay.

In Quebec, there is no government-sponsored fund to compensate victims of title fraud. Homebuyers and their lenders are able to rely on their notary's obligation to obtain valid interests in the property. Therefore, in the situation of fraud, the innocent victims could claim compensation from the notary's professional insurer. The victim would have to hire a lawyer to pursue the notary and his insurer for compensation and then pay to rectify title if it was stolen.

This is always the challenge: how to win back your own home after fraudsters have either mortgaged your property or actually stolen the title away from you. There seems to be no simple answer from the government, so protecting yourself is the best answer.

Title insurance operates on a no-fault basis. Once the insured owner or lender shows that their interest in the property is invalid based on fraud, the claim is established and paid by the insurer without cost to the insured. This section on the various provincial laws is merely a brief outline of the current situation. Those interested in more detail for their particular province should contact a real estate lawyer or the provincial law society.

The Best Remedy: Title Insurance

Despite the increasing number of high-profile real estate title fraud cases in Canada, many Canadian homeowners remain unaware of the best way to protect themselves against this crime. For two years, Environics Research has measured Canadian homeowners' knowledge and awareness of title insurance. The national survey asked approximately 1,500 Canadians whether they had protection in the form of title insurance for their home. Nearly half of homeowners over age forty-five said they do not have title insurance or are unaware if they do. The survey also found that 63% of Canadian homeowners without title insurance had absolutely no understanding of title insurance.[19]

Title insurance remains the only effective fraud protection tool available to the public today. The Land Assurance Funds across Canada need to add resources and processes to allow quick and responsive payouts to innocent Canadians caught in a fraudulent situation. How quickly they respond remains open to speculation. In the meantime, title insurance remains the best protection for recovery of the title to your property, where the law provides and will make immediate payment of legal costs incurred to recover it. In August 2006, on the topic of real estate fraud, the Canadian Association of Accredited Mortgage Professionals (CAAMP) stated that they recommend that the provinces promote the use of title insurance. They also stated that title insurance provides many benefits to borrowers and lenders.[20]

Susan Leslie, Vice President Claims and Underwriting at First Canadian Title, perhaps the most cited expert on title and mortgage fraud in Canada, told us the following:

Even with the recent changes in Canadian law relating to mortgage and title fraud, homeowners still benefit from title insurance upon falling victim to this crime; homeowners with title insurance will have the peace of mind that comes with turning the entire matter over to the title insurer.

The insurance company will hire experienced lawyers and investigators in order to quickly get to the heart of the matter. Homeowners will be spared the time and frustration of dealing with the various government departments and offices and the upfront costs of hiring lawyers and other experts in this area. Title insurers have the experience and knowledge required to quickly resolve the situation, by restoring title where appropriate and compensating for loss under a no-fault regime, all at the title insurers own expense.

Lenders are even more vulnerable, especially in Ontario, where the law now favours the innocent homeowner. Under Bill 152, lenders will be required to meet due diligence requirements before gaining access to the Fund. There are no guarantees for lenders, relating to expedited claims handling.

Real estate fraud is far too lucrative a crime for it to go away anytime soon. This crime will be with us for quite some time and we should be vigilant to all the signs and red flags we come across. Mortgage fraud starts with identity theft and then the fraudster impersonates the innocent victim in obtaining a mortgage or actually selling the original owners home without their knowledge. The victims might include the lender, the original homeowner, the innocent purchaser and all the individuals involved in the transaction from lawyer, to mortgage broker, to realtor.

Prevention of mortgage fraud requires the combined efforts of all parties to real estate and mortgage transactions because fraudsters will target the stage in the process where controls are lax. In addition, government, regulatory, and law enforcement efforts must recognize that mortgage fraud results in significant consequences for all victims.

Society, as a whole, pays for mortgage fraud. When it happens to you, however, the personal consequences become far more grave and complicated. An excellent resource is www.protectyourtitle.com, which is continually updated with current information on mortgage and title fraud.

The best advice we can give is to seriously consider title insurance on every home purchase and if you don't have it on your existing home already, buy it. The cost is very reasonable for the protection and peace of mind you receive for as long as you retain an interest in your home.

Chapter 6

Investment Fraud

George had belonged to his church for seventeen years and was a devout member of the congregation. He had been on many boards with the church and was keenly interested in enhancing his community. He was approached by an investment manager who had just started up a new ethical investment fund that invested only in companies that had a Christian-based portfolio and Christian philosophies. George was impressed with the manager and was equally impressed when he indicated he would guarantee a minimum of 12% return with the opportunity to make upwards of 40% per year.

George arranged a seminar series for the congregation to review this new ethical fund and the guaranteed approach to investing. The manager of the fund joined the church and became a devout member. Over the next two years, the members of this church invested over $18 million with this fund and George himself invested $40,000 of his savings.

During the first year, all investors where paid 21% return on their investment and they were simply delighted. The word spread among the church members of this great ethical investment and because fellow church members were doing so well, others wanted to participate.

The investment money flowed in, and for the next six months investors were rewarded with a 12% return. And then the interest cheques stopped coming. Promises were made to the congregation and still more people invested. By the end of the second year, it was clear something was wrong. The manager no longer returned phone calls, he no longer attended church, and his seminar series was cancelled.

The man had skipped town with all the investors' money. He had simply been taking a portion of the investment of others and paying it back to the members until he had amassed enough to leave town.

This is a simple fraud that exploits how we all like to trust others. Church members are targets of fraudsters because there is a natural trust among this community, and once that trust is established, money will follow.

Normal investment guidelines and research activities were not considered by these investors because of the promise of large returns, the trust they had for a fellow church member, and the fact that others had already been well paid in the first year. They all wanted to get on the bandwagon and reap the rewards. Greed overcame common sense, which is the stock and trade of the fraudster.

What Is Investment Fraud?

Investment fraud can be defined as an offer using fraudulent or false claims to solicit investments or loans, or providing for the purchase, use, or trade of forged or counterfeit securities. Fraudsters are coming from all directions offering "get rich quick" schemes and telling innocent victims that the returns are high and the risks are low. They also tell their prey: "The timing is right; you need to do it right away." These great but fraudulent offers may come by telephone, e-mail, or mail. More and more, they are coming via the Internet.

The "get rich quick" schemes and investment opportunities are a favourite of fraudsters, whether they are selling stocks, bonds, land, coin collections, etc. The main goal of the fraudster is to get you to invest as much of your money as possible.

Once they get you to invest, they come back for more. When you are duped out of your hard-earned money, there is one guarantee: you won't get anything back. The fraudsters are getting very creative in their approach to their victims as they send very attractive and official looking literature to tease and entice you into calling them or acting upon their requests. In recent years, the con artists have increased their use of unsolicited bulk e-mails (spam). The spam makes it extremely efficient for their schemes as it reaches millions of potential victims with the push of a button. The amount of spam that is currently being used to attract potential investors into fraudulent investment schemes is overwhelming.

Older persons are prime targets for phony investment brokers as these potential victims are geared towards securing their financial future. This, in addition to the fact that aging baby boomers are increasing in numbers, would suggest that the investment scams will show no signs of slowing down. Today, North Americans lose more than $40 billion a year to telemarketing fraud. Nest eggs are shrinking as older persons are seeing an increase in their cost of living for such items as medical expenses and general expenses around the house. With the increase in living expenses, the older person becomes even more vulnerable to scams and schemes that offer large returns with little so-called risks.

Year after year, millions of people of all ages worldwide lose their entire savings to the hands of unscrupulous swindlers who vanish without a trace. Whether you are young or old, there are numerous schemes to watch out for and there are many things you can do to avoid getting caught in a trap of deception and investment fraud. Some schemes may include the following: spam, phony websites, Ponzi schemes, pyramid schemes, misleading or false advertising, and boiler rooms. There are so many techniques used by con artists to access your money or assets but if you are aware of some of the more common techniques and how to protect yourself from these, you will hold onto your hard-earned assets and money.

Spam E-Mail Promoting Stocks

Spam is unsolicited e-mail that usually advertises or promotes a product, service, business, or scheme. Each setup is typically sent simultaneously to large numbers of e-mail addresses by people paid to promote a scheme. A growing proportion of spam e-mail is related to stocks. Con artists try to get you to buy stock in a certain company. You have no idea who they are and you have never heard of the company.

You should be wary of unsolicited e-mails that promote specific investments. Many of them promote microcap companies, which are smaller companies that often have limited assets. These microcap stocks often trade on the over-the-counter (OTC) markets. There are fewer regulations on the OTC markets than the major stock exchanges. These OTC markets include the United States OTC Bulletin Board (OTCBB) and the Pink Sheets.

The OTCBB is an American electronic quotation system that displays real-time quotes, sale prices, and trading information for stocks. Companies listed on the OTCBB must file financial reports with the United States Securities and Exchange Commission (SEC), but do not have to meet the listing requirements of the major exchanges. The Pink Sheets are listings of price quotes for companies that trade in the OTC market. The Pink Sheets are not regulated by Canadian securities regulators or the SEC.

All investments have some form of risk, but microcap stocks are considered high risk because many of these companies are new and have few assets or minor business operations. In addition, there is hardly any public information available about them. By contrast, larger public companies that trade on recognized exchanges such as the Toronto Stock Exchange (TSX) or the New York Stock Exchange (NYSE) must meet minimum listing requirements. To maintain a listing on the major exchanges, they must also file financial statements and other reports with securities regulators.

Nigerian 419 Spam E-Mail

Another popular spam e-mail is the West African Letter. This is also referred to the Nigerian 419 scam named for the violation of Section 419 of the Nigerian Criminal Code. The volume of e-mails that are sent out using this scam is overwhelming, and even when you block the sender and report the spam to your Internet service provider, the spam still seems to make it back again from another sender.

The con artists who send these e-mails portray themselves as high-ranking government officials or they may say they are close relatives of high-ranking officials. They usually claim to be from a developing country such as Nigeria. Their dilemma is quite outrageous as they have huge amounts of money (usually millions of dollars) languishing in a bank that they cannot access without the e-mail recipient's assistance. The story gets better: in return for the recipient's assistance, the con artist promises to pay a portion of money, which usually accounts for 20%.

In order to assist the con artist, the recipient of this e-mail is asked to deposit a sum of money in a bank account or to fax details of their own bank account. The con artist then proceeds to drain the victim's bank account. On March 20, 2007, *Dateline NBC* ran a segment on this topic, where they followed a con man and spoke to victims and the FBI. FBI agent John Hambrick stated, "At least ten thousand people will be victimized by this e-mail con this year alone."

Many of these e-mails claim to be from Nigeria, but they could be form anywhere in the world. The Government of

Nigeria and the Central Bank of Nigeria have been working towards a solution to stop this scheme. As they shut down one group, however, others replace them or they move to another country. It is extremely difficult for law enforcement agencies to track these criminals down. All it takes for the criminal to perpetrate this con is a computer with an Internet connection and a list of e-mail addresses.

Here is an example of a Nigerian 419 spam e-mail exactly the way it was sent and received:

I AM DR BASSEY OSSAI, SENIOR ADVOCATE OF NIGERIA(SAN). I REPRESENT MOHAMMED ABACHA, SON OF THE LATE GEN. SANI ABACHA, WHOWAS THE FORMER MILITARY HEAD OF STATE IN NIGERIA. HE DIED IN 1998. SINCEHIS DEATH, THE FAMILY HAS BEEN LOOSING A LOT OF MONEY DUE TO VINDICTIVEGOVERNMENT OFFICIALS WHO ARE BENT ON DEALING WITH THE FAMILY. BASED ON-THIS THEREFORE, THE FAMILY HAS ASKED ME TO SEEK FOR A FOREIGN PARTNER WHOCAN WORK WITH US AS TO MOVE OUT THE TOTAL SUM OF US$75,000,000.00 (SEVENTYFIVE MILLION UNITED STATES DOLLARS), PRESENTLY IN THEIR POSSESSION. THISMONEY WAS OF COURSE, ACQUIRED BY THE LATE PRESIDENT AND IS NOW KEPT SE-CRETLYBY THE FAMILY. THE SWISS GOVERNMENT HAS ALREADY FROZEN ALL THE ACCOUNTSOF THE FAMILY IN SWITZERLAND, AND SOME OTHER COUNTRIES WOULD SOON FOLLOWTO DO THE SAME. THIS BID BY SOME GOVERNMENT OFFI-CIALS TO DEAL WITH THISFAMILY HAS MADE IT NECESSARY THAT WE SEEK YOUR ASSISITANCE IN RECEIVING THIS MONEY AND IN INVESTING IT ON BEHALF OF THE FAMILY.

THIS MUST BE A JOINT VENTURE TRANSACTION

AND WE MUSTALL WORK TOGETHER. SINCE THIS MONEY IS STILL CASH, EXTRA SECURITYMEASURES HAVE BEEN TAKEN TO PROTECT IT FROM THEFT OR SEIZURE, PENDING WHENAGREEMENT IS REACHED ON WHEN AND HOW TO MOVE IT INTO ANY OF YOUR NOMINATEDBANK ACCOUNTS. I HAVE PERSONALLY WORKED OUT ALL MODALITIES FOR THE PEACEFULCONCLUSION OF THIS TRANSACTION. THE TRANSACTION DEFINITELY WOULD BE HANDLEDIN PHASES AND THE FIRST PHASE WILL INVOLVE THE MOVING OF US$25,000,000.00(TWENTY FIVE MILLION UNITED STATES DOLLARS). MY CLIENTS ARE WILLING TO-GIVE YOU A REASONABLE PERCENTAGE OF THIS MONEY AS SOON AS THE TRANSACTIONIS CONCLUDED. I WILL, HOWEVER, BASED ON THE GROUNDS THAT YOU ARE WILLINGTO WORK WITH US AND ALSO ALL CONTENTIOUS ISSUES DISCUSSED BEFORE THE COMMENCEMENTOF THIS TRANSACTION. YOU MAY ALSO DISCUSS YOUR PERCENTAGE BEFORE WE START TO WORK. AS SOON AS I HEAR FROM YOU, I WILL GIVE YOU ALL NECESSARY DETAILS AS TO HOW WE INTENDTO CARRY OUT THE WHOLE TRANSACTION. PLEASE, DO NOT ENTERTAIN ANY FEARS,AS ALL NECESSARY MODALITIES ARE IN PLACE, AND I ASSURE YOU OF ALL SUCCESSAND SAFETY IN THIS TRANSACTION.

PLEASE, THIS TRANSACTION REQUIRES ABSOLUTE CONFIDENTIALITYAND YOU WOULD BE EXPECTED TO TREAT IT AS SUCH UNTIL THE FUNDS ARE MOVEDOUT OF THIS COUNTRY. PLEASE, YOU WILL ALSO IGNORE THIS LETTER AND RESPECT OURTRUST IN YOU BY NOT EXPOSING THIS TRANSACTION, EVEN IF YOU ARE NOT INTERESTED.

YOU CAN CONTACT ME IMMEDIATELY ON TEL/FAX NUMBER 234 1775 3417 OR E-MAIL ADDRESS: IKEODILI@MAILCITY.COM .

I LOOK FORWARDS TO WORKING WITH YOU AND PRAY THAT THE YEAR 2000 WILL BRING US ALL BOUNTIFUL HARVEST.

THANK YOU,

DR BASSEY OSSAI

As you can see by the wording, the uppercase letters, and the request, it is truly a poor piece of work not worthy of a response. Here are some tips to avoid Nigerian 419 Fraud[21]:

- If you receive a letter from Nigeria (or any other country) asking you to send personal or banking information, do not reply in any manner.
- If you know someone who is corresponding in one of these schemes, encourage that person to contact law enforcement officials as soon as possible.
- Be skeptical of individuals representing themselves as Nigerian or foreign government officials asking for your help in placing large sums of money in overseas bank accounts.
- Do not believe the promise of large sums of money for your cooperation.
- Guard your account information carefully.

If you receive an unsolicited e-mail offering you an opportunity to get rich quick, you should treat this with suspicion. There are many other con games where the fraudster is trying to drain your bank account or deplete your assets. Some are promoting surefire stock tips or the latest multi-level marketing plan, while others offer easy access to locked-in assets. At the end of the day, there is only one person getting rich and it's not you.

It is highly recommended that investors protect themselves by researching all investment opportunities before investing. Investors should be particularly careful of spam e-mail, whether they are promoting get-rich-quick schemes or touting microcap investments. Microcaps, by their nature, can be very risky investments. While no investment is without risk, preliminary research might reduce the risk of investors falling victim to a scam or investing in something that doesn't meet their goals or drains their bank accounts. Here are some things you should watch out for:

• Unsolicited recommendations. How can someone who doesn't know you, your risk tolerance, and your financial objectives recommend a stock or investment? What are their real objectives? Why did they send you the unsolicited e-mail?

• Long wordy disclaimers and liberal use of jargon. Some spam e-mails have lengthy disclaimers that are quite different from other information in the e-mail. By reading the fine print, you might find that the people sending you the e-mail are being paid to promote the investment. They might also stand to benefit from an increase in the value of the investment they're encouraging you to purchase. They will likely use financial jargon to convince you that the people or company behind the opportunity are professional, knowledgeable and experienced. This information should not be taken seriously.

• High-pressure sales tactics. A spam e-mail will urge you to act, using statements like "This one is ready to explode!" and "We have a winner—opportunities like this don't come around every day." The reason they push you is they are trying to influence the value of the investment.

Here's what you should do if you receive spam:

- Don't reply. If you reply to the sender to remove you from their mailing list, that tells them that they have a legitimate e-mail address and you could get more spam.

- Delete the e-mail. Use the "block sender" or "bounce" features in your e-mail message tools. Report the e-mail as "junk" e-mail to your Internet service provider. This helps the service provider to increase the effectiveness of junk mail filters and can reduce the amount of spam you receive in the future.

Phony Websites

Investment fraud can also arise through the use of phony websites seeking to trap investors. The Ontario Securities Commission has warned investors to be on the lookout for phony websites claiming to be security regulators. You should do a thorough investigation before submitting any personal information to any website. It is very easy to verify if an organization is real or phony and the due diligence you perform upfront could save you money and reduce stress. You don't want your personal information in the wrong hands. Many phony websites claiming to be security regulators have been using the fake site to gather information on investors so they can lure them into investment schemes. This form of phishing and pharming was covered in greater detail in Chapter 4: Internet and E-mail Fraud. According to the North American Securities Administrators Association (NASAA) there are numerous "phantom regulators" that have been targeting investors worldwide so they can endorse their fraudulent investment opportunities.

It's a good idea to investigate further to make sure you are dealing with the right agency or commission. Some signs that a regulator may be a "phantom"[22]:

- You can't find references to the organization on any other regulatory websites, and legitimate regulators have never heard of them. In Canada, check with the securities regulator in your province or territory. For contact information, see the Canadian Securities Administrators website: www.csa-acvm.ca.

- They endorse or promote any particular investment opportunity. A legitimate regulator would never do this.

- They claim that paying a fee to "release restricted shares" is not an attempt to steal your savings. This is a common ploy and a recent twist on age-old advance fee schemes. For more information or to report a suspected phantom regulator, please contact your securities regulator outlined in the appendix "Provincial and Territorial Securities Regulators." For free educational resources on how to protect you from frauds and scams, you can also visit the www.investorED.ca website.

Ponzi Schemes

A Ponzi scheme is an investment fraud where the fraudster promises high returns or dividends that are not normally available through traditional investments. The operator never invests the victims' funds. Instead, the operator pays "dividends" to the initial investors, using the original amounts "invested" by subsequent investors. The story at the beginning of this chapter about the church group that was swindled out of millions of dollars is a typical Ponzi scheme. The scheme generally falls apart when the con artist takes off with all of the proceeds or when a sufficient number of new investors cannot be found to permit the continued payment of "dividends." Robbing from Peter to pay Paul is the master plan.

Recently, a British Columbia man was accused of helping to finance terrorist activities through a Ponzi scheme. He raised over $14 million from 352 investors by promising to invest their money in businesses, commodities, and financial instruments. The securities commission in B.C claimed he used funds of new investors to pay interest to previous investors. This fraudster was also accused of similar activity in the United States and Ontario. This type of scheme is often successful because the promise of high returns can make it hard to refuse.

You need to be wary of promises that sound too good to be true. All legitimate investments have some degree of risk that makes it difficult to promise astronomical returns. It is always wise to seek the advice of a licensed professional investment advisor prior to making any investments. They have the knowledge, experience and the tools to do the due diligence required prior to making an investment. You should also be wary of hard-sell tactics that have any sense of urgency. There should never be any pressure to "act now!" "If you snooze, you lose" is not a good omen; ignore those sales pitches completely.

Pyramid Schemes

Pyramid schemes are sometimes referred to as franchise fraud, multi-level marketing (MLM), or chain referral schemes. These are marketing and investment frauds in which an individual is offered a distributorship or franchise to market a particular product or service.

Multi-level marketing is a system of selling in which you recruit people to assist you and they, in turn, sign up others to help them, and so on. Some entrepreneurs have built successful companies on this concept and their businesses are thriving today because the main focus of their activities is their product and sales. There are numerous MLM companies, such as Isagenix, Mary Kay, Avon, and Tupperware, which currently run very successfully with great products and services and have no connection to fraudulent activity at all.

There are, however, many multi-level schemes that are just sophisticated chain letters. These schemes operate as a "pyramid," claiming participants can earn lots of money by concentrating all of their efforts on recruiting distributors rather than selling a product or service.

All members of a pyramid are successful when they constantly recruit more people to join the distributorship. There are only so many people who can be recruited and only so many products or services that can be sold. It is also very hard to control all of the individuals within the distributorship. In addition, some may be motivated and some may have joined through a high-pressure sales tactic and may not be motivated. The cost to enter a pyramid could be quite high and it is normally considered lost once you pay.

It is important to do your research before you join any franchise, distributorship, or multi-level marketing organization to verify if the company is legitimate. Is the company geared towards recruiting or selling a product or service? Protect yourself and your money by doing your homework first. Multi-level marketing schemes and illegal pyramid schemes don't offer the path to wealth, so try to avoid them.

Advertisements Promoting Investment Opportunities

There are numerous fraudsters placing advertisements who might not be properly registered to trade in securities. As well, some of these ads provide misleading information to the public regarding potential investments. These appear in many types of media, including newspapers, television, radio, magazines, newsletters, and the Internet. As mentioned previously, Internet spam is becoming a popular way to promote investments.

The investments described in the advertisements look authentic, but unless investors verify this first with an objective source such as their financial advisor, banker, accountant, or provincial/territorial securities regulator, they could risk committing their money to an illegitimate investment. Once you hand over your money, it's extremely difficult for investors to get it back.

Regardless of the source, we urge investors to protect themselves by researching all investment opportunities before investing. As most investors are aware, no investment is without risk. If you do your research in advance, you can lessen the risk of falling victim to an investment scheme. Just because something looks good and authentic, it doesn't mean it is. Appearances can be deceiving, so you should be cautious before you write the cheque. Here are some things you should watch for[23]:

- Promises of low risk and high return. Ads may promote quick and above-average growth and "guaranteed security." When someone offers above-average growth involving little risk on your part, you should always question this.

- Liberal use of financial jargon. Sometimes, ads use sophisticated language to convince investors that the people behind the opportunity are professional, knowledgeable, and experienced. Anyone can use financial lingo to sound convincing, so don't take it at face value. Do your research to verify the facts.

- Free seminars and workshops. In addition to promoting free registration, the ad may offer the public additional incentives, such as free food, gifts, etc., for participating. Be cautious if you attend one of these sessions. The session might focus on investing or tax-savings strategies or it could end up promoting a specific investment. Don't commit until you've checked into the person or firm offering the opportunity. There are many legitimate seminars being held daily, across Canada, by reputable speakers and investment professionals, so it is important to recognize which are legitimate and which are scams.

- High-pressure sales tactics. Some ads will urge you to invest while the opportunity's hot and to act now. You should never feel pressured to invest. Good opportunities will be there long enough for you to check into it first to make sure it's legitimate.

- Company's alleged track record. Many ads promote the fact that the company or person offering the opportunity has been in business a long time, are backed by a large corporation, and/or have achieved high performance in years past. A company's track record should never be the sole deciding factor when making an investment decision. You should research the company's history and track record but also take into account other factors such as your investment objectives before committing to an investment.

- Requests for personal information. Ads may send you to a toll-free line, website, or a free seminar so you can request more information or fill out an application form. Check to ensure the investment opportunity is legitimate before submitting information. If it is a potential scam, your personal information could be shared, sold, or held for use in future scams. The personal information, as we have mentioned many times before, could also be used to steal your identity.

- Tax savings or tax-shelter incentives. Be wary of advertisements that promote tax-saving incentives, especially leading into tax season. Promoters could use a toll-free number, website, or free seminar to promote how the tax savings work. Promoters who tell investors that a tax shelter identification number means the shelter has been approved by Canada Revenue Agency (CRA) are misleading investors. The identification number is actually for identification purposes only and it does not in any way confirm the entitlement of an investor to claim any tax benefits associated with any tax shelters.

Canadians should be cautious when a promoter tries to sell an investment using charitable donations that promises a tax receipt for more than the amount you paid. The CRA regularly audits these schemes. Recently, they uncovered a scheme that involved millions of dollars being funnelled through a church in Ontario. The investors or donators in this scheme will probably be reassessed for all or most of their receipt value. Again, always do your homework before you get involved with any kind of scheme that sounds too good to be true!

Boiler Rooms

Getting an unsolicited telephone call about an investment opportunity could mean you are a target of a boiler room operation, the kind of which have returned once again across Canada. Boiler room operators are notorious for offering promises of quick profits, but the only ones who actually profit from this is the con artists and it's all at your expense. They never offer any investments that you can benefit from and are only involved for their sole benefit. Many of the boiler room operations are located in the main financial district of a major city near other large well-known firms, but the actual address may only be a small rented space out of the public's sight. You have to ask yourself, "Why would a complete stranger call to offer you a no-risk, high-return investment?"

The boiler room salesperson is very good at gaining your trust as they smooth-talk you into believing they have access to an investment that is only available through them and it's something so good that you have to buy it quickly before it's no longer available. The investment could be tied to a medical breakthrough for detecting a highly untreatable disease or something that can reduce the amount of fuel your car consumes. They go right after your heart and your wallet. Your investment in their offering could help bring the product to the marketplace and eventually lead to a public offering. "Watch the stock value soar!" they tell you. Most of the time, the investment is sold with promises of quick profits, which makes the return on your investment look real good. If the offer is so good, why do they have to do cold calls to strangers to attract investors?

Here are some tips to avoid becoming a victim of a boiler room:

- High-pressure sales. Always research all investment opportunities. If you are not sure, get a second opinion.
- High returns and no-risk promises. If an investment offers a return higher than the current norm for conventional investments, then the risks could also mean bigger losses.
- Setup calls. The first call will offer information to tweak your interest about the investment. This setup is priming you for the next call, which is the pressured sales pitch.
- Unregistered salespersons. Verify if the salesperson is licensed to sell the investment they are offering you. Call your securities regulator (see appendix 6, Provincial and Territorial Securities Regulators, for the list) to confirm their registration and services they are permitted to offer.

If you are suspicious about a scam or if you have been swindled by a boiler room operation, you should contact your local law enforcement agency as well as the provincial regulator. It is crucial that you gather as much information as possible: the caller's name, the company's name, the investment, and the date and time of the call(s). The more information you collect, the better. If you report the scams you can assist in closing down the boiler rooms and prevent someone from getting scammed again.

Red Flags of Potential Investment Fraud

It is really important to be cautious of strangers offering you something that sounds too good to be true. If you are not sure about an offer or an investment opportunity, please review it with a friend, a banker, a lawyer, an accountant, or your financial advisor. Here is a summary of red flags that should cause you to reflect and investigate prior to acting:

- Promises of high-return, low-risk investment opportunities
- Unsolicited calls
- Loans to access locked-in RRSP funds
- Promotion of offshore tax havens
- Unregistered salespeople
- Tax savings or tax shelters
- Opportunities to invest in a company that's about to go public
- Requests for help in transferring funds
- Unsolicited e-mail messages, also known as "spam"
- Suggestions of swapping recognized blue chip stocks for worthless stocks
- Investment is limited to accredited investors, but exceptions will be made for you
- Promise of huge profits with little effort
- Non-disclosure agreements
- Schemes involving recruiting of others
- High-pressure sales tactics
- Requests for personal information
- Company's purported track record
- Use of confusing financial jargon

Some of these may be legitimate, but more than likely they are not. Full disclosure in writing is always a good test of someone's honest intentions, but even that can be misleading some times.

Protect Your Money and Investments

- Be wary of unsolicited offers received via the Internet, mail, or telephone.
- Check the registration and background of the person or company offering you the investment.
- Don't invest in anything based on appearances. Just because an individual or company has a flashy website, it doesn't mean it's legitimate. Websites can be created in a matter of minutes. After a short period of taking money, a site can vanish without a trace.
- Don't invest in anything you are not absolutely sure about. Do your homework on the investment to ensure that it is legitimate.
- Check out other websites regarding this person or company.
- Be cautious when responding to special investment offers (especially through unsolicited e-mail).
- Be cautious when dealing with individuals or companies from outside your own country. Inquire about all the terms and conditions.
- Take your time in making a decision to invest—don't rush into a "high-profit, low risk" offer.
- Get all information in writing before you consider investing.
- Check out the firm by calling the Better Business Bureau or by looking them up in the local phone book.
- Never sign documents you have not read or that do not meet your financial goals.
- Never complete a form with false information. You

should not deal with a person who asks you to do that, nor should you accept their investment advice.

If you are prudent and wise, you can avoid investment fraud. Be wary of promises of quick profits, offers to share "inside" information, and pressures to invest before you have an opportunity to investigate and research the investment. Protecting your hard-earned money and assets is important, but it becomes more important as you get older. Without your money and assets, it would be hard to survive in today's society. Don't let embarrassment or fear keep you from reporting investment fraud.

Chapter 7

Telephone Fraud

One of us received a call. It went like this: "This is Peter and I'm calling from the Security Department at MasterCard. My badge identification number is 76154. Our records show your card has been flagged for an abnormal purchase pattern, and I'm calling to authenticate. This would be on your MasterCard, which was issued by your bank. Did you purchase an anti-telemarketing device for $397.99 from an online marketing company based in California?"

I replied, "No."

The caller next said, "Then we will be issuing a credit to your MasterCard account for that amount. We have been watching this company for a while now, especially for charges ranging from $249 to $499, just under the $500 purchase pattern that flags most cards. Before your next statement, the credit for $397.99 will be mailed to (he repeated my address). Is that correct?"

After I confirmed the address, the caller said, "I will be starting a thorough fraud investigation. If you have any questions, you should call the 1-800 number listed on the back of your card and ask for the Security Department. You will need to refer to the file control number 76154-01432."

I wrote down the number and then he said he needed to verify that I was in possession of my card. He instructed me to turn my card over and look for some numbers. He said, "There are sixteen numbers. These are the major part of your card number; the next three are the security numbers that verify you are the possessor of the card. These numbers are sometimes used to make Internet purchases to prove you have the card."

He asked me to read to him the three numbers, which I did. He said, "That's correct, I just wanted to verify that the card has not been lost or stolen and that you still have your card." He was very pleasant about the whole thing. He thanked me and said, "Don't hesitate to call back if you need anything," and hung up.

After that phone call, I noticed numerous charges on my credit card statement that I didn't make. I don't know how they originally got my card number and address, but I gave them the three-digit number to help them make online purchases. This is just one of thousands of deceptive phone calls that are being made daily on unsuspecting consumers throughout North America and around the world. The estimated losses by Canadians are in millions and in the United States it is in the billions.

According to PhoneBusters, the Canadian anti-fraud call centre, the use of telephones to market goods and services (telemarketing) has expanded dramatically over recent years. Sales in Canada now exceed $500 billion a year, but not all of these telemarketing activities are legitimate. Unfortunately, criminals use many similar telemarketing techniques to defraud consumers.

PhoneBusters also says that since the early '70s, deceptive telemarketing practices have been a problem in Canada, with numerous cross-border implications. Telemarketing fraud has now become one of the most pervasive forms of white-collar crime. Not all crimes are reported by the victims, so it is hard to estimate the true numbers and value of these crimes.[24] Deceptive telemarketing occurs when someone uses the phone to obtain payment from you for a misrepresented or non-existent product, service, or charitable gift. It also occurs when someone uses the phone to obtain your personal banking information or steals your credit card number from you. Offering you a prize for which you must pay a fee is deceptive telemarketing. Any time someone uses the phone to obtain your money fraudulently in any way it is deceptive telemarketing. This is a serious crime and it is punishable by jail.

Criminals are drawn to this crime by large proceeds and relatively low risks of detection, prosecution, and punishment. The fines and the imprisonment are relatively low compared to the large bounty obtained through this criminal activity. Since the '80s, low-cost telecommunications have created economies of scale and provided fraudsters with effective means of conducting potentially massive frauds. A single telemarketer with a well-organized scheme can easily extort several hundred thousand dollars per year from unsuspecting victims. In some cases, the high profits have also attracted organized crime.

Target Victims and Groups

The criminals select their victims with a strategy in mind. They don't choose at random but with a calculated plan to target groups that are the most vulnerable. The groups that telemarketers tend to target the most are seniors. This group usually has more assets and savings as well as an open ear to listen to the telemarketer's sales pitch. Some of these seniors actually enjoy the conversation and are quite polite and responsive to the telemarketers. These seniors could be added to a "sucker list" and sold off to another telemarketer and targeted all over again.

Recognizing Telephone Fraud

The most common telephone deceptions come by fax, voice mail, and incoming calls. How can you recognize a phone scam? The best thing to remember at all times is the following: If it sounds too good to be true, it probably is! Telephone con artists will sometimes tell you that you have won a great prize in a contest you don't remember entering...that's a good clue.

Another clue you are being scammed would be the following: You are told you are a winner of something, but to claim the prize you must send money in advance...not a cheque, but a money order payable to cash. You have no idea why you won something and now they want you to pay to get the winning prize! They will tell you that they need the cash to pay for duties, processing, or taxes. Paying in advance like this is outright illegal and you should never follow through with a request like that.

Many new schemes involve the phishing for personal and confidential information. When someone calls to request this information, they usually pretend to be your bank, a government agency, or insurance company. This process of disguising themselves as another person to extract your personal information is called pre-texting. Many of the sophisticated pre-texting schemes involve a return phone number. This level of sophistication is well organized and usually involves a phone tree, where you are redirected to the right person. They set it up in such a way that you really believe you are dealing with a large, reputable organization, making it seem legitimate. You should never reply to pre-texting phone calls. Your financial institution will never contact you in such a way. (Please seen Chapter 4: Internet and E-Mail Fraud for more detail.) If you think a request for personal information is legitimate, contact the institution by using the phone number on your credit card, on your credit card statement, or on their website; make sure it is their website and not a spoofed site. When you are dealing with a possible pre-texting phone scam, be sure to ask to whom you are talking and take note of as many details as possible. This information will be very useful and essential if you are a victim of identity theft and you need to file a police report or an Identity Theft Statement. (See appendix.)

Another way to identify a phone fraud is by the way the caller acts on the phone. If they seem unusually excited about the offer they have, this is a good signal of a potential fraud scam. If they want to be your best friend, I would also be suspicious of their actions. Some criminals will try to find out if you are lonely, and once they know that, they will attempt to bond with you and convince you they are your best friend. This is all about gaining your trust so they can perpetrate the scam.

The best defense against phone fraud is to *hang up!* It's not rude to do this; it's the intelligent thing to do. Also, as a general rule, always be cautious with whom you share personal information.

Toll-Free Telephone Number Scams

There are numerous companies that charge for calls to 800, 888, and other toll-free numbers. These companies usually offer audio entertainment or information services and the charge for the call is how they obtain the revenue to run the service. In order for a company to bill you for these calls, they must obtain your agreement in advance for the billing arrangement and they must detail all the pertinent information about the rates. The company's name, address, and telephone contact number must be outlined in the agreement as well. Here's how to minimize your risk of unauthorized charges[25]:

• Remember that dialling a number that begins with 888 is just like dialling an 800 number; both are often toll-free, but not always. Companies are prohibited from charging you for calls to these numbers unless they set up a valid agreement with you first.

• Recognize that not all numbers beginning with "8" are toll-free. For example, the area code 809 serves the Dominican Republic. If you dial this area code, you'll be charged international long-distance rates.

• Check your phone bill for 800, 888, or unfamiliar charges. Calls to 800 and 888 numbers should be identified. Some may be mislabelled as "long distance" or "calling card" calls and are easy to overlook.

• Dispute charges on your phone bill for an 800 or 888 number if you don't have an arrangement. Follow the instructions on your billing statement.

Realize that if the telephone company removes a charge for an 800- or 888-number call, the entertainment or information service provider may try to pursue the charge through a collection agency.

900 Scams
The 900 telephone number scams can be a very expensive experience if you don't catch them right away. These schemes are similar to the prize-pitch telephone scams as the consumer will receive an offer via the mail that will encourage them to call the 900 number to find out what type of prize they have won. The con artists will entice you to respond by offering a small gift if you call. The major problem with this call is the cost per minute, which adds up while you find out how small the prize actually is. If you have any questions or concerns about a 900 number, immediately contact PhoneBusters at 1 (888) 495-8501 or www.phonebusters.com. PhoneBusters is a national anti-fraud call centre operated by the Ontario Provin-

cial Police and the RCMP. It is the central agency that collects information on telemarketing and identity theft complaints.

Tips for Recognizing Telephone Fraud

- The offer is too good to be true.
- You won a contest you never entered.
- You must pay to play.
- The need for private and personal information.
- Request for cash or money order.
- The caller is far more excited than you are.
- It's the manager calling.
- Stranger wants to be your best friend.
- Limited opportunity.
- You must act quickly.

Tips for Avoiding Telephone Fraud

- Ask the telemarketers for a phone number that you can call them back on.
- Ask the caller to send written information regarding their offer or product.
- Call the local Better Business Bureau (BBB) to verify the company's status. (See the appendix for a complete list of all the BBBs across Canada.)
- Talk to a family member, friend, financial advisor, accountant, banker, or lawyer before handing over large amounts of cash for a purchase made over the phone with a stranger.
- Don't pay any fees in advance for a prize you have supposedly won.
- Don't be pressured into acting quickly on a purchase.
- Shop around and compare before you buy.
- Use only the numbers listed on the back of your credit card, statement, or the listed phone number.

- Do not use the number listed on an e-mail or left on a voice message; verify first.
- Never be fooled by promises of special offers, prizes, or large amounts of money.
- Never share personal information such as bank accounts, credit card information, social insurance number, or PINs over the phone. Your bank will never ask for that over the phone.
- Report all fraudulent activity to the police immediately.
- Sign up for the "Do Not Contact Service," which is operated by the Canadian Marketing Association (www.cmaconsumersense.org).
- Use common sense and be cautious of strangers who call you unsolicited.
- Ask them to stop calling or just *hang up!*

Chapter 8

Fraud against Seniors

On May 21, 2007, the *Toronto Star* published an article written by Charles Duhigg of the *New York Times* on a probe being conducted by the RCMP that involved seniors being scammed out of hundreds of thousands of dollars. The thieves were operating out of offices in Toronto and rooms the size of airplane hangers in India. The targets of the telemarketing con artists were war veterans, retired teachers, and other elderly persons. The scam was one of the oldest techniques used to dupe seniors out of their money.

The *Toronto Star* reported that the telemarketers would pose as government officials and insurance company workers and ask the seniors for information needed to update their files. Loaded with the information they acquired, the fraudsters then emptied the seniors' bank accounts. According to the article, one retired army veteran lost more than $100,000. Many of the people who were conned into giving up their personal information had entered a sweepstakes contest in the past and had then given out enough information to start a list by the sweepstakes organizers. The list was then sold to good and bad marketers. In this case, the unscrupulous telemarketers used the list to complete the con. The veteran who lost the $100,000, told the *New York Times* reporter that he loved receiving the calls because he was lonely since his wife passed away. Being confined to his home with arthritis, he spent most of his time filling out sweepstakes, organizing his mail, and listening to big band music while he chatted with telemarketers.[26]

Seniors constitute one of the fastest growing population groups in Canada. The 2001 Census revealed that there were nearly four million seniors aged sixty-five years and older, accounting for 13% of Canada's population. Projections indicate that by 2031, seniors will comprise between 23 and 25% of the Canadian population. Ageing baby boomers, low fertility rates, and an increase in life expectancy will all contribute to the expected doubling of the proportion of seniors over the next twenty-five years.[27]

Most of the baby boomers who are starting to enter into the senior citizen category are in better financial health than most of their previous generations. As we advance in medical technology, we are also seeing life expectancy increasing at higher levels. All of this is great news for the aging society. It hasn't, however, gone unnoticed by the criminals who love to target seniors and their assets.

Knowing this, corporate Canada and our neighbours to the south are gearing up their services, products, and marketing machine in order to capitalize on the changing demographics. Seniors have been targeted by fraudsters for many years with many schemes and it doesn't appear as though this situation is subsiding. As this group grows, there will always be some seedy con artist trying some new or old scheme to alleviate the senior victim of their hard-earned savings and assets. In North America, nearly 30% of all fraud victims are seniors.

If you are approaching the age of retirement or you have a relative, friend, or neighbour who is a senior citizen, you should watch for warning signs as you would not want yourself or your acquaintances to be put in jeopardy. Scam artists claim that their success with elderly victims is based on many factors. Those who have been caught, claim that the seniors are quite easy to talk to and they have success in gaining their trust as many of them are lonely, especially those who live alone. Sometimes the telemarketer may be the only voice they hear in a day or even a week at a time. The con artist telemarketer ends up building trust over time to the point where it may get as strong as a blood relative's trust. The telemarketer works toward this strong relationship so they can go for as much money as possible and, in some cases, completely drain their senior victim's bank account.

There are other methods used to locate and draw out senior victims. One of the more common tools, other than the telephone, is the mail. Most of us look at our junk mail and throw it in the trash immediately, while seniors do the opposite. The seniors become more vulnerable when they open all the mail they receive, and the con artists know this. With their flashy marketing pieces, they go right after seniors' hearts and wallets. Soon after, it's not unusual to hear that a senior relative has spent thousands of dollars associated with the pursuit of a major prize associated with some kind of lottery or so-called sweepstakes.

The con artists know the right strings to pull, and once the senior has been lured into their maze, through the telephone or mail, it is difficult to escape without some financial setback. Looking for warning signs and helping an older relative or friend avoid a scam is the right thing to do.

Another popular arena for fraud is the Internet. As baby boomers become seniors, they will carry forward their good Internet security habits, but some of them will get a little lax and that could cause a whole new trend of fraud as e-mail and Internet usage grows. As we mentioned in Chapter 4: Internet and E-mail Fraud, there are many ways you can lose your personal information and assets. It is important to always follow the steps outlined in that chapter to maintain a safe and reliable Internet experience.

Seniors are always concerned about their economic security and their consumer protection; however, this is constantly being compromised by a continuous wave of criminal scams that threaten their financial security, safety, and independence. In addition to telemarketing and investment fraud, which we covered in greater detail earlier, here is a list of some other threats to the well-being of most seniors:

- Fraudulent sweepstakes or lotteries
- Charitable solicitation
- Funeral plans
- Home-repair fraud
- Medical fraud
- Exploitation from caregivers, friends, and relatives

Billions of dollars are lost across North America through fraudulent activities, and the border between us and our American neighbours is a very thin line when fraud is cultivated. The fraudsters don't see the border when they target seniors and other age groups. They will continue to target seniors because of weak laws and the short sentences given to those who commit the crimes. The losses through fraud can be devastating. This is especially the case for older victims who have may have left the workforce and are on a fixed income.

With age comes wisdom and experience, but this is not always enough to stop fraudsters and con artists from targeting seniors. We compiled a list of the most significant reasons why seniors are targeted and are at risk. Seniors reading this list will see how vulnerable they could be. If you are aware that con artists are trying to steal your personal information, assets, and money, you will be better prepared to protect yourself.

Why Fraudsters Target Seniors[28]

- More trusting. Today's seniors are from an era when people trusted their neighbours and local businesses. Many are less skeptical of fraudulent activities and even strangers!

- More leisure time. People are living longer and many are retiring earlier. This extra time can easily turn into empty hours that can simply be filled with reading mail, taking phone calls, responding to unsolicited advertisements on the Internet, or responding to door-to-door solicitations from strangers offering great deals on renovations, low-risk investments, and great prizes.

- Have assets available. Seniors have built up their net worth to include bank accounts, home equity, RRSPs, and insurance proceeds.

- Isolated and lonely. Many elderly victims are widowed, live alone, or do not have grown children or other support networks that look in on them or help attend to their affairs. They also feel isolated by rapidly changing technology that they don't understand and by relatives and family members who don't have as much time for them.

- Anxiety. With the increase in life expectancy and the effects of inflation, seniors are often concerned about not having enough money to maintain their lifestyle. Some are also concerned about not having an inheritance for their children and loved ones.

- Reluctant to seek assistance. Seniors are reluctant to contact the proper authorities to help protect themselves because of many factors such as embarrassment from being duped, the need to feel independent, health issues, and the reluctance to turn supposed trusted friends and even family members in to the police.

- Sometimes willing to take financial risk. Some seniors are willing to take on financial risk to address their financial needs for health care in the hope of leaving a larger financial legacy for the children.

Other Factors That Aggravate the Problem[29]

- Diminishing police resources. Low recruitment and budget-controlled governments have resulted in less manpower allocated to crimes that do not involve violence. Fraud below a certain threshold ($10,000 to $25,000) is not often investigated, allowing the criminals the freedom to work without fear of severe consequences.

- Criminals are aging. With the baby boomers pushing their way through the generations, so too are the number of criminals in that same age group. These criminals have the same mindset, education, capability, and resources to commit identity theft and many forms of fraud.

- Jurisdiction issues. With the advances of technology, fraudsters and con artists operate in areas outside of local jurisdictions. The difficulty of cross-border investigations and prosecution is often beyond local police departments' resources.

- Low-risk activity. Identity theft pays out on average approximately $3,000 per incident and about $30,000 per identity, with a low risk of personal harm or incarceration compared to robbing a bank, which nets a similar amount of money.

- Under-reporting. Individuals don't report out of embarrassment and fear of humiliation. Seniors also fear losing their independence in self-management of their financial affairs. Companies are very conscious of their image and will often just release an employee rather than go through the publicity associated with prosecution.

Types of Financial Exploitation of the Elderly

As mentioned previously, a senior can be a victim of many forms of fraud. Many of these schemes are solicitations by phone, face to face, mail, and the Internet. Some of the most common are:

- Sweepstakes, contests, and prize promotions. Many telephone and direct-mail contests seldom let seniors win. Some are so bold as to ask for an advance fee to play and they also make exaggerated promises and claims.

- Investments and other business opportunities. There are numerous fraudulent investment scams for businesses, multi-level marketing schemes, and franchises that target seniors with their false claims of high profits with little risk. We covered more on this topic in Chapter 6: Investment Fraud.

- Travel and vacations. Free trips or discounted travel is offered to seniors that never materialize. Why would someone offer you such a great deal? We are all tempted by the offer of free or discounted travel.

- Home repair. Fraudulent contractors charge inflated prices and do little or no work after they take the senior's money upfront. An example of a plumbing fraud includes replacing an entire toilet when the problem could have been resolved by running a metallic snake through the pipes. Another example of fraud would include such things as replacing the entire eavestrough when only the corners needed replacing or patching. It's wise to use home contractors referred by close friends, neighbours, and family. Always get a quote upfront and don't be afraid to ask others for advice prior to committing to the work. If you don't feel comfortable with the workers, call a friend or family member to check out the situation before your give up too much of your money. Never pay for the entire job upfront. Small deposits are fine, but be careful they don't run off with your deposit and leave you with no work done at all!

- Charitable solicitations. Many fraudulent charities solicit money for their own personal use and not for the charity they claim to represent. With their legitimate-sounding names, they con seniors into donating money that was destined for other needy groups or organizations. We cover this topic in greater detail in Chapter 9: Other Fraud.

- Caretaker fraud. This is fraudulent activity carried out by those given the task and trust of taking care of the elderly, such as a family member or healthcare worker from an institution or hospital. This type of fraud ranges from theft of valuables and money to overbilling for services. When you trust someone that close to you and they perpetrate these crimes, it can be a very emotional and heartbreaking situation, which can leave the elderly victim unable to trust anyone in the future.

    This is one of the worst kinds of fraud because it is perpetrated by those the elderly highly trust. There have been cases of identity theft by family members who set up false power of attorney to sell the elderly person's home without their consent while they are in the care of an institution.

Documents are forged, assets are stolen, and identities are taken without the knowledge of the elderly. If you have a family member under the care of someone at home or in an institution, you should watch for unusual circumstances surrounding their banking, investments, personal belongings, wills, power of attorney, and any other items that may involve assets or access to these assets.

No matter what you do or where you go, you should always protect your personal information and your assets. Be wise and educate yourself before you entrust someone.

Wired Seniors

Most people sixty-five and older do not go online very much, but when the Internet-loving baby boomers start to turn sixty-five, there will be an online "silver tsunami." This huge demographic shift may bring some areas of concern, as the older Internet users could attract some unfriendly elements such as viruses, spyware, and other online intrusions. Some of these issues may also lead to fraudulent activities when seniors let their guard down.

As the senior population goes online, they should always be aware of the many threats on the Internet, whether it be through e-mail, shopping, or browsing. As we mentioned in Chapter 4: Internet and E-Mail Fraud, you need to keep up to date with antivirus software, anti-spyware, and always have a firewall active on your computer. If you want to educate yourself on how to be safe on the Internet, www.onguardonline.gov is a great American website that is tailor-made for seniors. It covers scams, shopping, viruses, spam, spyware, and more. The website was launched in September 2005 by the Federal Trade Commission and it can be a great first stop for senior citizens and others concerned about using the Internet safely. The site uses multimedia for this interactive education and it can help seniors stay safe online.

Providing Assistance to Senior Fraud Victims

We need to take care of our senior relatives and friends because they usually have difficulty being their own advocates when they are victims of fraud. As victims of non-violent crimes such as fraud and theft, they are hurt in many ways beyond their finances. The pain from these crimes can be emotionally as well as spiritually devastating and may even cause physical effects. With more and more elderly living on fixed incomes, or even below the poverty line, fraud could cause them to go without some of the basic necessities such as food or medicine. The elderly should be enjoying life with their grandchildren while conserving their assets and not suffering any financial difficulty caused by a con artist's schemes. The loss of assets and money can cause the elderly to suffer permanent and sometimes life-threatening setbacks. The relatives of elderly victims may also feel the pain and suffering when they are called upon to support the relative emotionally and sometimes financially. It now becomes a role reversal, where children are now taking care of their parents.

Warning Signs of Fraudulent Behaviour[30]

- A marked increase in the amount of mail with too-good-to-be-true offers, including lots of junk mail for contests, free trips, prizes, sweepstakes, and lotteries.

- A house crowded with cheap items such as costume jewellery, watches, pens, small appliances, radios, beauty products, plastic cameras, vitamins, water filters, or other items purchased in order to "win" something or received as "valuable prizes."

- Numerous calls and requests for multiple contributions to the same charities or to several charities that do not seem to be of interest to the contributor.

- Secretive behaviour regarding numerous telephone calls throughout the day that are long in duration.

- Receiving unsolicited phone calls from fast-talking operators offering "fantastic" opportunities to claim prizes or make sure-fire investments.

- Chequing account shows escalating withdrawals to unfamiliar, out-of-province destinations, or several cheques issued to the same companies or duplicate payments for the same orders.

- Payments being picked up by private or commercial couriers or being wired.

- Sudden and inexplicable money-related problems buying food or paying bills.

- Requests for loans or cash.

- Many magazines or books of inappropriate subject matter for the reader's interests (e.g. *Young Bride*, *Extreme Surfing*).

- Books on how to enter and win sweepstakes.

- A sudden, unexpected loss in their bank account.

- Tells you about frequent calls from "nice folks" offering prizes, investment opportunities, or requesting charitable donations.

- Makes repeated and/or large payments to unknown companies.

- Unexpected or incomplete repairs done on their home.

- Explains to you how an organization is offering to help recover money they paid to a telemarketer—for a fee.

If you suspect that someone you know has fallen prey to a deceptive telemarketer, fraudulent caregiver, con-artist repairman, or Internet scam, don't criticize them for being naive. Avoid blame and don't call them stupid, greedy, or foolish and don't lecture them. Try to think of them and not your lost inheritance. Avoid threatening to take over their personal finances as that may backfire—they may become even more secretive and very resentful. It is better to point out the seriousness of the crime and that reporting the fraud to the authorities will assist in stopping this from happening to someone else. Encourage them to share their concerns with you about unsolicited calls or any new business or charitable dealings. Assure them that it is not rude to hang up on suspicious calls. You could also offer to go over their bank and credit card statements to see that only authorized transactions are listed.

Avoiding Con-Artist Schemes

It is estimated that over 50% of the names on telemarketers' lists of the most likely victims are individuals aged fifty years or older. Seniors need to be especially vigilant and knowledgeable of con artist and fraud schemes. Seniors are often targeted because they usually have an accumulation of assets, may live alone, are likely interested in saving money, live on a fixed income, and are more easily reached by phone or are at home during the day.

Below are some prevention tips to help you avoid being targeted by a con artist.[31] As you review these ideas, think about how you or your senior relatives and friends are most vulnerable and try to counter these temptations and security lapses with a few of your own best tactics.

- Beware of any program or offer that seems to give you something for nothing. As we have said before, if it sounds too good to be true, it probably is.

- Beware of free prizes that require a credit card number for verification with your three-digit security number. Never give your credit card number over the phone unless you have made the call and are dealing with a reputable business that you have done business with before. We covered many aspects of credit card security in Chapter 2: Debit and Credit Card Fraud.

- Do not give out any personal information about yourself (i.e. address, phone number, bank information, Social Insurance Number, etc.) to anyone over the phone or in person whom you did not contact yourself.

- If you are interested in a deal, give yourself 24 hours to think it over. The time you spend thinking about the idea will be time well spent. Ask a friend, relative, banker, financial advisor, lawyer, or accountant to review the business offer.

- Do not be pressured to take action immediately. Asking someone to "act now" is a high-pressure sales tactic. If it's a good buy right now, it will be a good buy tomorrow.

- Ask for information on any product or service you are considering in writing and read it over carefully. Read the fine print closely (it might require a magnifier, but go ahead and use it). Ask a friend or family member to read it as well. Two sets of eyes and experiences can make all the difference in the world.

- Do not return mail-order solicitations because these provide information about you that can be shared with telemarketers and others.

- If door-to-door salespeople approach your home, do not answer the door or let them in. If you do let them in and they will not leave, call the police. Do not be afraid to say, "No."

- Arrange for the direct deposit of any cheques you regularly receive by mail.

- Never provide personal information such as account or credit card numbers over the computer unless you are 100% sure it is the valid and safe Internet site that you selected. If you arrived at the site through a link in an e-mail, it could be a spoofed site.

- Only give to charities you know and trust.

- Never rush into something involving your money or property.

- Always get a few estimates. Ask someone to review the estimates before you make a cash outlay.

- Be wary of "something for nothing" or "get rich quick" schemes.

- Never turn over large sums of money to anybody, especially a stranger, no matter how promising the deal looks.

- If pressured by a salesperson, refuse to be bullied and say, "No thanks." Walk away, close the door, hang up the phone—it's your right!

- Do not hesitate to check the credentials of a salesperson or public official.

- Know that your signature is negotiable. Only sign contracts or cheques after you've read them and you're certain it's for a legitimate reason.

- Report suspicious offers or activities to the police immediately.

What to Do for the Victim

If you suspect that you or someone you know has been a victim of fraud or a stolen purse or wallet, contact your local police immediately. You don't have to be embarrassed or ashamed. If possible, write down any important information while it's still fresh in your memory. If you have any questions or concerns about safety or want to get actively involved in crime prevention, contact your local police service or RCMP. You will be doing the right thing and hopefully getting the fraudster out of business and out of your neighbourhood.

Chapter 9

Other Fraud

Congratulations! You Won! (Or So You Think)

Over the past few years, there has been a substantial increase in the number of e-mails claiming that people have won extremely large sums of money in an international lottery or sweepstakes. These official looking unsolicited e-mails come from remote parts of the world and they arrive with lots of fanfare telling the receiver that they must claim their grand prize as soon as possible. They also claim that the prize has been deposited with a financial security firm and if you want to claim the money, you need to do a few things first: 1) don't tell anyone until you receive the money, and 2) send an e-mail to their claims agent.

All of this sounds a little fishy and quite unusual. How did you win a contest you never entered? In order to claim your award, you need to send money to the fraudsters who in turn will open up your file for processing the grand prize. If you don't send money in advance, you can't receive the prize. In addition to this advance fee, the claims agent will also ask you for personal information such as your Social Insurance Number, bank account number, and credit card information. They tell you that they need this confidential information to perform credit checks, but they are in the process of robbing you.

People that follow-up with these fraudsters are being swept away by the dreams and fantasies of winning a large jackpot. Who doesn't dream of winning the lottery and what they would do with all that money? Besides e-mail, fraudulent lottery schemes can arrive in the mail or you may be contacted by phone.

In addition to the lottery and sweepstakes scams, many consumers have been receiving calls from people claiming to be from reputable retailers. They claim that they have a special "reward" for their loyal customers and that they need a payment upfront before they can send the reward. This is an example of an advance-fee scam.

We all love to win—may it be a coffee while rolling up the rim to win, a free lottery ticket, or the hockey pool at work. When the potential prize is larger, we sometimes lose our common sense. We need to be more cautious, especially when dealing with complete strangers and especially when we are told we have won a contest we never entered. Here are some useful tips to remember if you receive a telephone call, e-mail, or letter announcing that you have won a prize, cash award, lottery, or sweepstakes:

- Are you being asked to send money in advance, provide financial information such as bank accounts, or credit card details so you can claim your winnings? Any of these could be a scheme to steal your money, assets, or even your identity.

- Official regulated lotteries and sweepstakes companies never require their contest winners to pay any fees in advance. You should never pay for taxes, courier, or any other fees prior to receiving your winnings.

- Will you ever actually be entered into the company's sweepstakes? Chances are you won't. They also are prohibited by law to require you to buy something to enter a contest or receive sweepstakes mailings.

- The fine print on the sweepstakes offer or entry form will probably outline various outcomes that clearly state what happens if you win or if your number is selected. Just because you receive the offer or entry form, it doesn't mean you have won anything yet.

- Don't be fooled by official sounding and official looking offers with gold seals and awards, even if they clam to be endorsed by a government agency within Canada or from another country. By law, a promoter is not permitted to represent themselves being affiliated with any government agency.

- If you respond to any fraudulent sweepstakes, you may open the floodgates for more unsolicited bogus offers. The best thing to do is completely ignore any mail or e-mail contests and report the telemarketing fraudsters to PhoneBusters at 1-888-495-8501 or by e-mail at info@phonebusters.com.

- Don't give out any personal information over the phone, by mail or over the Internet to anyone unless you know who you are dealing with and you have verified that they truly are the person or company you want to deal with.

Nobody running a legitimate organization would ever ask you to pay up front for a lottery or sweepstakes, especially when you never entered. If they are asking for personal information they are up to no good. Remember the war veteran who lost $100,000 completing sweepstakes forms on a regular basis.

Advance Fee for Loan Schemes

If you've ever had difficulty getting a loan through normal lending channels, you may have become a target of an advance-fee loan scheme. In this type of scheme, the con artist guarantees your loan but only if you pay a fee in advance. The fraudsters claim they can secure the loan through a reputable lender such as a well-known bank or credit union. The con artist, however, is not able to do this at all. They are very good at disappearing after they have taken your fee. Some are bold enough to stick around and go after more victims while they stall you with false excuses. The advance fee is usually 5% of the total loan request. A loan of $5,000 could have an advance fee of $250. Be careful not to get caught paying any fees as they can add up quickly if you lose your guard.

You should ask yourself (and the con artist), "Why can they get me a loan from a reputable lender when I couldn't myself?" You should also protect your personal information when asked to pay any upfront fees for a loan. The con artist may be setting you up for more than a loan. With all of your personal information on the loan application, a sophisticated con artist can recreate your identity and start a whole new round of problems for you.

Tips to Avoid Advance Fee for Loan Schemes

The following tips will help you avoid being victimized by an advance-fee swindler if you are not dealing directly with a lending institution on your own behalf:

- Get as much information as possible about the loan representative and their company. You should always know with whom you are dealing.
- Never accept anyone's guarantee that a loan will be completed unless it is with a reputable lender such as a bank or credit union.

- Verify with whom the promoter will be procuring the loan and ask that particular lender for details of the loan.
- Get local references from the promoter and confirm whether they got what they paid for.
- Consider consulting a lawyer, financial advisor, or accountant for advice.

Don't fall prey to fraudsters asking for any fees prior to delivery of your loan. The same should be said for renovation deposits. If you are asked for a deposit for any kind of home renovation, it is recommended you verify the background of the contractor and get everything in writing. Dealing with someone you know through a referral and having a comfort zone will make it easier to let go of that initial deposit.

Another form of advance-fee scams is the Nigerian 419, which we discussed previously in Chapter 6: Investment Fraud. This scam started in the mid-'90s when people were asked to pay a fee upfront to be able to access a Nigerian prince's bank account. It has evolved into one of the most aggressive e-mail scams in the world. The RCMP estimates that Canadians have lost in excess of $30 million to this scam over the past ten years. It doesn't have to be from Nigeria to qualify for this type of scam. The fraudsters are using all types of reasons to get the advance fees and the e-mails are coming from all over the world. The basic premise is the demand for money upfront so you can have access to larger sums of money afterward. As in most cases, why would you give money to a complete stranger?

Charity Fraud

Charity fraud happens when a group or individual solicits charitable funds for phony causes or deliberately misrepresents its fundraising intentions. Frequently throughout the year, and more often during the holiday season, you probably get appeals in the mail or by telephone urging you to contribute financially to a good cause. There are currently in excess of 82,000 charities in Canada. According to an article published in the *Toronto Star* on June 2, 2007, donors in Canada give approximately $40 billion a year to charities. This is a combination of tax-receipted donations, payments through lotteries, membership dues, and other sources related to charities. Charitable fraud is so big that the Canada Revenue Agency has a team of forty auditors working in this area exclusively. The vast majority of charities do good work, but there are many that don't.

Disasters, whether natural or manmade, are great opportunities for people to come together and help those in need. Unfortunately, there is always a criminal element lurking in the background, trying to capitalize on the situation. Fraudulent websites with the intention of steering funds away from legitimate fundraising organizations pop up very quickly after these disasters. The Internet has become a very popular format for gathering funds for legitimate and fraudulent charities. The con artists will prey on the generosity and vulnerability of people and capitalize on this during times of crisis or disaster.

The last thing on the mind of fraudsters scheming for your money is charity; they have one intention: take the money intended for the needy and put it into their own hands. Who is legitimate and who isn't? If you receive a solicitation from an unknown charity, you should do some research before you donate. Find out who they are, how they will use your donation, what percentage goes to administration of the charity, and how much gets used for the actual "good work." By choosing a well-known recognized charity, you can ensure that your donation reaches the proper destination and is used for its intended purpose.

In Canada, the most recognized charity is the Canadian Red Cross. There are many other legitimate charitable organizations, but before you donate, be sure they are who they say they are.

Charity Checklist

You should consider the following safety measures to ensure that your charitable donation dollars benefit those people, groups, and organizations you want to assist. These are good practices whether you're contacted by mail, phone, or in person.[32]

- If the person says, "Thank you for last year's donation," but you never made a donation to that group before, be cautious. Be on the alert for invoices claiming you've made a pledge. Some unscrupulous solicitors use this approach to get your money.

- Be wary of appeals that tug at your heartstrings such as those involving current events and patriotism.

- Ask for a callback number. If they can't provide a callback number, hang up.

- Ask for written information about the charity, including name, address, telephone number, and registration number. If they don't provide this information or you can't verify this information, do not donate. A legitimate charity or fundraiser will always give you information about the charity's goals and mission and how your charitable donation will be used.

- Ask for a receipt showing the amount of the contribution and stating it is tax deductible.

- Be wary of requests to support police or firefighters. Some fraudulent fundraisers claim the donations will benefit these groups when, in fact, little or no money goes to them at all. Contact your local fire or police department to verify that the fundraising is legitimate and what percentage actually goes to them.

- Check out the charity's financial information. For many charitable organizations, this information can be found online or you can ask them to e-mail, fax, or mail it to you.

- Ask for identification. If the solicitor refuses to tell you or does not have some form or verifiable identification, hang up or close the door and report it to local law enforcement officials.

- Call the charity directly. Verify if the organization is aware of the solicitation and has authorized the use of its name. If not, you might be dealing with a scam artist.

- Watch out for similar sounding names. Some phony charities use names that closely resemble those of respected, legitimate organizations. If you notice a small difference from the name of the charity you intend to deal with, call the organization you know to check it out.

- Ask how your donation will be distributed. How much will go to the program you want to support (as opposed to other programs of the non-profit) and how much will cover the charity's administrative and telemarketing costs?

- Don't provide personal information over the phone. Be concerned if the person asking for donation starts asking for personal information about you, your family, your maiden name, or who lives with you.

- Refuse high-pressure appeals. Legitimate fundraisers won't push you to give on the spot.

- Be wary of charities offering to send a courier or

overnight delivery service to collect your donation immediately.

- Consider the costs. When buying merchandise or tickets for special events, or when receiving "free" goods in exchange for giving, remember that these items cost money and are generally paid for out of your contribution. Although this can be an effective fundraising tool, less money will be available to the charity.

- Be wary of guaranteed sweepstakes winnings in exchange for a contribution. According to law, you never have to donate anything to be eligible to win.

- If the telemarketer claims that the charity will support a local organization, call the local group to verify. Check out the credentials of the fundraiser against the ones given by the local group to match the company engaged to raise the money for the local group.

- Be wary of e-mails that ask for charitable donations since most legitimate charities don't solicit money this way.

- Avoid cash gifts. Cash can be lost or stolen. For security and tax purposes, it's best to pay by cheque.

- Discuss the donation with a trusted family member, financial advisor, or friend before committing the funds.

Faith-Based Investment Scams

Investment scams that take advantage of spiritual and religious beliefs are another form of fraud and they are on the rise. In some of these situations, the unsuspecting victims are sold bogus promissory notes and in others, they are being promised rates of returns well above the norm. There has also been a return of the classic Ponzi scheme, where new investors are continuously solicited to make interest or divided payments to previous investors. We covered the Ponzi scheme in greater detail in Chapter 6 on Investment Fraud. Just because someone is a member of your congregation doesn't make them an investment specialist who can turn your hard earned money into gold! The North American Securities Administrators Association (NASAA) estimates that over the last three years, about 90,000 Americans have lost roughly $1.8 billion to frauds that use religion as a lure.[33]

Con artists who use religion to promote their scams often:

- Use the Bible to predict financial or social crises;
- Make claims that they will reinvest part of their profits to a charitable organization; and
- State that your belief and support in their scam equates to faith in your religion.

Before making any investment, we suggest investors consider the following:

- Did you receive and review the prospectus before you bought the investment and was the information contained in this document clear enough for you to understand? Did you review all written information with your financial advisor, accountant, or lawyer prior to purchasing the investment?
- Are the claims for the return on your investment realistic?
- Whether you have an investment strategy for your risk tolerance or not, you should ensure that the investment fits your goals.

Medical Fraud

Another form of fraud that goes right to the consumer's heart is the medical fraud scheme. Many fraudsters are taking advantage of people with medical issues such as cancer, diabetes and obesity. In recent years, the Canadian Government has announced collaborative actions in association with Mexico and the United States to combat this type of fraud.

According to Health Canada, in a press release issued on October 24, 2005[34]:

> Companies are promoting bogus and misleading weight-loss schemes that endanger health, provide false hope, and defraud their citizens of billions of dollars. Fighting weight-loss fraud is a key priority for all three countries, as unprecedented numbers of citizens of all ages have become either overweight or obese, and this trend shows no sign of abating. According to the World Health Organization, more than 60% of American and Mexican citizens and more than 50% of Canadians are overweight or obese. Obesity and being overweight are major contributors to chronic disease and disability. These conditions pose major long-term public health risks requiring proven and effective treatments, not diet products or programs that do not deliver the promised results. These fraudulent products and programs target vulnerable consumers and simply don't work.
>
> Consumers are quite vulnerable when it is a question of evaluating health product claims. They want to lose weight and they want to believe that a product will work for them. Now, through the Internet, these claims are not just coming from our own country but from elsewhere. Weight-loss scams account for a large proportion of global health fraud and prey on consumers who are often desperate for a solution to their weight problems.
>
> Billions of dollars are spent on ineffective and sometimes dangerous weight-loss products and schemes promoted by fraudulent advertisers.

It is important to note that before you try a new diet or lifestyle change to lose weight, you should always consult a doctor. Most professionals will remind consumers that the only way to lose weight is to lower caloric intake and/or increase physical activity.

Approximately two million Canadians of all ages are affected by diabetes. This is a serious health issue that affects a large number of people all over the world and many consumers are lured by false claims about miracle cures for this disease. Any product that claims to be a miracle cure for diabetes is a fraud that could cheat Canadians of their time, money, and, most important, their health. Government agencies from Mexico, United States, and Canada are trying to stop medical fraud by deterring false and misleading diabetes cure-all advertising and labelling, including Internet sweeps, warnings, recalls, seizures, import refusals, prosecutions, and other enforcement actions.

Due to the cross-border nature of Internet fraud, there needs to be an international response. The message to consumers is: be smart, be skeptical. If it sounds too good to be true, it likely is.

Criminal Charges Laid in Cancer Treatment Scam Following Competition Bureau Investigation

On August 2, 2005, the Competition Bureau announced that criminal charges were laid against Michael Reynolds of Toronto, Ontario, and John Armstrong of Penticton, British Columbia, for making false or misleading claims regarding the efficacy of their alleged cancer treatment.[35] The principals of the now defunct CSCT Inc., operating out of Kitchener, Ontario, and Penticton, claimed that their treatment, originally known as Cell Specific Cancer Therapy (later known as Zoetron Therapy), could selectively kill cancer cells without harming healthy cells.

The Competition Bureau alleged that the accused preyed

upon vulnerable consumers, specifically cancer victims and/or their families, by making unsubstantiated representations on their website, at seminars, and in alternative health-care magazine articles and advertisements, direct mailings, and telephone communications. The two accused operated their outpatient cancer clinics in Santo Domingo, Dominican Republic; Tijuana, Mexico; Lausanne, Switzerland; and Mijas Costa, Spain, at various times from August 1996 to February 2003.

The accused claimed to have treated over 850 people worldwide, while charging as much as $15,000 to $20,000 (U.S.) for the alleged treatment. This did not include substantial additional expenses incurred by victims and their families, including international travel and accommodation. The monetary loss, while significant, is overshadowed by the false hope created by the accused that those in need of serious medical treatment would receive help.

This investigation was conducted with the assistance of various agencies, including The Toronto Strategic Partnership, a law enforcement partnership established to combat cross-border telemarketing fraud. Its membership consists of the Toronto Police Service, Ontario Provincial Police, York Regional Police, RCMP, Ontario Ministry of Consumer and Business Services, U.S. Federal Trade Commission, U.S. Postal Inspection Service and U.K. Office of Fair Trading. Assistance was also received from law enforcement officials in Switzerland, Belgium, and Spain.

These enforcement actions effectively shut down the operation. There are numerous medical fraud operations actively duping people out of their life savings while giving them a false sense of hope for "the cure." With assistance from the public, we can stop these fraudsters. Try not to support these organizations unless you have strong, verifiable proof that the cure works. It's best to rely on modern medicine and local doctors for the remedies that cure us.

As we have mentioned throughout the book, it is really important that you do your research before you let go of your money and your personal information. There is always someone out their trying to steal your money, whether it be through a fraudulent charity, a cure that doesn't deliver, a fake website, a con artist's e-mail, or the chance to win something big or make large profits quickly. Be cautious at all times.

Appendix 1

Identity Theft Statement Instructions

If you have been a victim of identity theft, the Identity Theft Statement helps you notify financial institutions, credit card issuers, and other companies about the incident. It tells them that you did not create the debt or charges and gives them information they need to begin an investigation. Make as many copies of the statement as you will need to notify all affected companies.

The Identity Theft Statement consists of two parts:

- Part One: Identity Theft Statement. This part asks for general information about you and the identity theft.

- Part Two: Statement of Unauthorized Account Activity. This part asks you for specific information about accounts or activities. Complete this section specifically for each company you're notifying, and send each company only the information that relates to accounts or activities with that company.

Once you have completed and signed the statement, attach copies (not originals) of any supporting documents you have (e.g. transaction records, receipts, a police report). Keep a copy of everything that you are submitting for your own records.

Provide the completed statement and attached documents to each financial institution, credit card issuer, or other company that provided the identity thief with unauthorized credit or money. Send the documents by registered mail or courier, or deliver them in person, so that you can prove that they were received. The companies will review the information and will contact you to let you know the outcome of their investigation or to obtain further information.

The statement and supporting materials will contain important information about you, so they should be kept in a safe place and should only be shared with the companies and law enforcement agencies that require the information.

Completing the Identity Theft Statement does not guarantee that the identity thief will be prosecuted or that the debt or charges will be cleared. Each company will determine whether to absolve you of the charges or debt. Note that if you are seeking reimbursement for any loss, you may need to provide separate forms or documents, and reimbursement will be subject to applicable policies and account agreements.

This statement is only intended for companies that give you credit and other services. Please do not send the Identity Theft Statement to a government department or ministry.

The following list includes financial institutions, credit card issuers, and other companies that accept the Identity Theft Statement. This list may not be exhaustive. If you are reporting identity theft to a company that is not listed below, ask the company if they accept the statement.

Amex Bank of Canada
1-866-216-5388

ING Direct
1-888-464-1111

BMO Financial Group
1-800-363-9922

President's Choice Financial
1-888-723-888

CIBC
Contact your branch

President's Choice Financial
MasterCard
1-866-246-7262

Canadian Tire Financial
Services
1-800-965-5585

RBC Financial Group
Contact your branch

Citibank Canada
1-800-387-1616

Scotiabank
1-800-813-6602

CitiFinancial Canada
1-888-622-8766

Sears Canada Inc.
1-800-565-3460

Desjardins Credit Union
Contact your branch

TD Bank Financial Group
Contact your branch

HBC Hudson's Bay Company
1-800-263-2599

The following list names additional organizations that have a role in fighting identity theft or protecting consumers. These organizations endorse the Identity Theft Statement as a useful tool for a person who has been a victim of identity theft.

Canadian Association of Chiefs of Police
Canadian Bankers Association
Canadian Council of Better Business Bureaus

Consumers' Association of Canada
Consumers Council of Canada
Credit Counselling Canada
Equifax Canada
MasterCard Canada
Ontario Association of Credit Counselling Services
PhoneBusters National Call Centre
Public Interest Advocacy Centre
Retail Council of Canada
TransUnion Canada
Volunteer Centre of Toronto—ABCs of Fraud Program
Visa Canada

Appendix 2

Identity Theft Statement

Identity Theft Statement

To: _____

(Name of financial institution, credit card issuer, or other company)

Part One: Information about You and the Incident

I, _____ , state as follows:

Personal Information

1) My full legal name is:
_____

(First)   (Middle)   (Last)

2) My commonly-used name (if different from above) is:
_____

(First)   (Middle)   (Last)

3) My date of birth is:
(year/month/day):_____/_____/_____

4) My address is: _____

City: _____Province/Territory: _____Postal Code: ___

5) My home phone number is:_____

6) My business phone number is: _____

7) I prefer to be contacted at:
❑   Home:
❑   Business:
❑   Alternate number: _____

Name: _____

Information about the Incident
Please check all that apply:

❒ 8) ☐ I became aware of the incident through:

_____
_____
_____
_____
_____
_____
_____
_____

❒ 9) I did not authorize anyone to use my name or personal information to seek the money, credit, loans, goods or services described in this document.

❒ 10) I did not receive any benefit, money goods or services as a result of the events described in this document.

❒ 11) My identification documents(s), (e.g. driver's license, passport, SIN card, birth certificate) were:

_____Lost on or about (y/m/d)_____ /_____ /_____
_____Stolen on or about (y/m/d)_____ /_____ /_____
_____Never received

Additional information (e.g. which cards, circumstances):

_____
_____
_____

Name: _____

☐ 12) Additional Comments (for example, a description of the incident, what information was used or how a possible identity thief gained access to your information):

_____

_____

_____

_____

_____

(Attach additional pages as necessary)

This information notifies companies that an incident has occurred and it allows them to investigate your claim. Depending on the details of your case, each company may need to contact you with further questions.

Investigation and Enforcement Information

☐ 13) I have reported the events described in this document to the police or another law enforcement agency.

In the event that you have contacted the police or another law enforcement agency, please complete the following:

_____

Agency   Officer

_____

Phone Number   Badge Number

_____

Date of Report   Report Number, if any

Name: _____

Documentation

Please indicate the supporting documentation you are able to provide. Attach legible copies (not originals) to this document.

❏ 14) A copy of the report completed by the Police or law enforcement agency (if available).

❏ 15) Other supporting documentation (describe):

_____
_____
_____
_____
_____
_____
_____
_____
_____

Name: _____

Part Two: Statement of Unauthorized Account Activity

Complete this section separately for each company you are notifying.

❏ The account(s) described in the following table (e.g. deposit account, savings account, credit card account) was/were opened at your company in my name without my knowledge, authorization or consent, using my personal information or identifying documents.

❏ My account(s) described in the following table (e.g. deposit account, savings account, credit card account) was/were accessed, used, or debited without my knowledge, authorization or consent, using my personal information or identifying documents.

The unauthorized activity took place through (if known):
❏ An in-person transaction
❏ An automated banking machine (ABM/ATM)
❏ A point of sale purchase
❏ A telephone transaction
❏ A cheque
❏ Other _____
❏ Don't know

❏ The credit product(s) described in the following table (e.g. loan, mortgage, line of credit) was/were obtained from your company in my name without my knowledge, authorization or consent, using my personal information or identifying documents.

Name: _____

Description of Unauthorized Account Activity

Company Name/Address	Type of Account/ Account Number	Description of unauthorized activity (if known)	Date (if known)	Amount (if known)
Example: ABC Bank, 123 Street, Any town	Deposit Account 1234567-890	Withdrawal or: all activity since 10/01/02	10/01/06	$500

Attach additional pages as needed

If the incident involved a mortgage, please indicate:

Lender's Name/ Address	Date of (if known)	Legal description of the property	Municipal Address of the property	Registration Number of mortgage (if known)

Attach additional pages as needed

❐ During the time of the incident(s) described above, I had
   the following account(s) opened with your company
   (*please list any account not mentioned above*):

Billing Name _____

Billing Address _____

Account/Card Number _____

Name: _____

Protecting your Privacy

I agree that companies to whom I provide the Identity Theft Statement may use the personal information in it only for the purposes of investigating the incident described in the Statement, prosecuting the person(s) responsible and preventing further fraud or theft. The companies may disclose the information to law enforcement institutions or agencies (for example, police departments) for these purposes.

The companies to whom I provide the Identity Theft Statement agree that this information may not be used or disclosed for any other purposes except as authorized by law. If this document or information contained in it is requested in a law enforcement proceeding (e.g. before a court or tribunal), the company may have to provide it or disclose it.

All statements I have made on this form are true and complete in every respect to the best of my knowledge and belief.

_____   _____
Signature   Signature of Witness (not
                                 immediate family)

_____   _____
Printed Name   Printed Name

_____   _____
Date   Date

                                 _____
                                 Telephone Number

Knowingly submitting false information in this statement could subject you to criminal prosecution.

The Identy Theft Statement can be downloaded at
www.phonebusters.com.

Appendix 3

Credit Reporting Agencies

Equifax
Call 1-800-465-7166 to place a fraud alert.
www.equifax.ca

Equifax Credit Information Services
P.O. Box 190, Station Jean-Talon
Montreal, Quebec, H1S 2Z2

TransUnion
Call 1-800-663-9980 (Quebec residents 1-877-713-3393) to
place a fraud alert.
www.transunion.com

TransUnion Fraud Victim Assistance Department
P.O. Box 338, LCD1
Hamilton, Ontario, L8L 7W2

Residents of Quebec contact:
TransUnion Fraud Victim Assistance Department
1 Place Laval, Suite 370
Laval, Quebec, H7N 1A1

Experian
1-888-826-1718
www.creditbureaus.ca
Experian Canada's Fraud Victim Assistance Department
Fax: 1-800-646-5876

Experian
P.O. Box 727
Rouyn-Noranda, Quebec, J9X 5C6

Appendix 4

Real Estate Lawyer Checklist

This checklist was put together by Stephen Shub and is used on a regular basis by his office, which operates a law practice that concentrates predominately on real estate transactions. The objective of the list is to assist in verifying that all the details of a real estate deal are accurate and that there are no fraudulent activities taking place on the transaction.

Checklist:
Initial conversation with clients regarding use of "Power of Attorney"

Refinance File
Power of Attorney (POA) to be used: yes ☐ no ☐
   If yes, explain reason: _____
POA exists now ☐ to be prepared by _____
We have original POA in our files: yes ☐ no ☐
Client told we need a POA by fax plus original to close:
                                  yes ☐ no ☐
Received owner's Photo ID with second ID and handwritten note currently dated confirming Canadian residency and

POA still valid and okay to use, signed by owner, faxed to
us directly: yes ❐ no ❐

Client warned we need direct telephone # to donor:
yes ❐ no ❐

Client warned proceeds only paid to registered owner:
yes ❐ no ❐

Sale File

Will all registered owners be available to attend for final sign-
up? yes ❐ no ❐

If no, explain: _____

If POA being used: Client warned money only paid to registered owner: yes ❐ no ❐

Client warned we need photo ID, faxed with current dated
and signed note that POA still valid and okay to use for
sale: yes ❐ no ❐

Client warned we need direct telephone # to client:
yes ❐ no ❐

Client warned we need faxed copy ASAP: yes ❐ no ❐

Originally signed POA for closing: yes ❐ no ❐

Client confirms being Canadian resident: yes ❐ no ❐

If no, client warned re: 25% non-resident trust holdback until
clearance obtained: yes ❐ no ❐

Pre-Closing Checklist re: "Power of Attorney"
Sale File

❐ Power of Attorney used

❐ Photo ID of owner obtained and signed note to S. Shub
by owner re: okay to sell and POA still valid

❐ Donor of POA phoned to confirm POA circumstance if
POA not done in our office

❐ Signature on note compared okay with POA signature

❐ POA checked okay re: name(s) of registered owner(s)

❐ Two witnesses on POA (Not spouse or immediate family)

❑ No restrictions preventing use for sale closing
❑ Original or notarial copy of POA obtained
❑ Registration of POA noted on disbursement sheet
❑ E-Reg documents to register POA prepared
❑ Yellow highlight placed on closing list to register POA before transfer released

Refinance File
If Power of Attorney Being Used:
❑ Photo ID of owner and second ID obtained with current dated and signed note to S. Shub by owner re: okay to use POA for financing and POA still valid
❑ Donor of POA phoned to confirm POA circumstances if POA not done in our office
❑ Signature on note compared okay with POA signature
❑ POA checked okay re: names of registered owner(s); re: two witnesses; re: no restrictions preventing use of mortgage refinancing
❑ Original or notarial copy of POA obtained
❑ Registration of POA noted on disbursement sheet
❑ E-Reg document to register POA prepared
❑ Yellow highlight placed on closing list to register POA before mortgage

Fraud Flags in Pre-Closing Routine
Sales File
❑ Suspicious Circumstances: sub file created if new client *not* buying and substantial net $ to new client.
❑ S. Shub told

Fraud flags if private sale:
We acted for vendor before: yes ❑ no ❑
Rush closing: yes ❑ no ❑
www.411.ca checked re: clients telephone # connects to address sold or to identifiable address: yes ❑ no ❑

Deposits paid to lawyer in trust: yes ❐ no ❐

Call client to confirm client can easily provide all usual documents: yes ❐ no ❐

Ontario driver's license and passport okay for sign up and funds to be paid to registered owner okay:

      yes ❐ no ❐

If no vendor stated, problem is:_____

❐ *Fraud Flags* (if no mortgage to discharge):

Copy of register obtained showing deleted instruments checked re: any mortgage discharge in last six months: no recent mortgage discharge ❐ or recent mortgage discharge is: # _____

Refinance File

❐ Suspicious circumstances:

Sub file created if new client *not* buying and substantial net $ to new client: yes ❐ no ❐ S. Shub told ❐

❐ Fraud flags review: if two or more "yes" answers on initial consultation, S. Shub has been consulted and S. Shub said okay to proceed _____ (S. Shub initials)

❐ Fraud flags review (after title search):

If no mortgage to be discharged, deleted instruments show mortgage discharged in last six months: yes ❐ no ❐

Title transfer occurred in last six months and we did *not* act for client   yes ❐ no ❐

If YES to any above matters: S. Shub told ❐; S. Shub initialed okay to proceed _____ (initial)

Purchase File

❐ *Fraud Flags*: (if private deal): deposit paid to Lawyer in trust: yes ❐ no ❐; if no, S. Shub advised ❐

❐ Fraud Flags Review (after title search):

If *no* mortgage to be discharged *and* deleted instruments show mortgage discharged in last six months yes: ❐ N/A ❐

Vendor is not one of registered owners   yes: ❐ N/A ❐

Non-Builder title transfer occurred in last twelve months at
    much lower price: yes: ❐ N/A ❐

❐ If yes, noted in mortgage paragraph

❐ If yes to any above matters: S. Shub told

Did vendor solicitor act for vendor when bought:

                yes ❐ no ❐ N/A ❐

Fraud flag letter sent to vendor solicitor: yes ❐ no ❐

❐ If act for mortgagee:

❐ Instructions highlighted

❐ Conditions in mortgage checked

❐ Conditions taped to subfield

Mortgagor(s) and Covenanter(s) names checked okay ❐; or
    discrepancy is _____

❐ E-Reg Mortgage direction prepared

❐ Acknowledgement direction prepared

❐ Interim report sent

❐ Insurance binder received showing mortgagee

❐ Fax sent to mortgagee re: non builder transfer in last year

❐ Fax to mortgagee if added deposit direction to vendor or
    if large closing credit to principle in excess of $3,500

❐ Mortgagor same as transferees

❐ Okay to release advance

Review of Photo ID on Signup with Client:

❐ Copy of photo ID obtained (two forms of ID if mortgage)

❐ Unexpired okay

❐ Any discrepancy between name on photo ID with name
    on registered ownership noted

❐ Photo appears okay

❐ Signature on photo ID reasonably compared to signature
    on documents being signed

Suspicious Circumstances (Yes / No)

If there will be substantial net proceeds (from a sale or a mortgage refinance) to be paid to client (who is not using funds to buy and who was not previously known by our office), consider the following matters to help determine whether the transaction might be fraudulent:

1) Have we acted for the client before? If so, for what type of matter? A fraudster typically does not return to the same lawyer who did prior work.

2) Is the closing a rush closing, is the client being anxious for the law office to close quickly? A fraudster is anxious to close quickly (to hit and run) so that the innocent duped lawyer, who is the tool of the fraudster, has no time to think before filling the fraudster's pocket (it is easier than robbing a bank and fraudulent ID is easy to purchase). The fraudster's own picture and signature will usually appear on the fraudulent ID, which will reflect the name of the true registered owner.

3) Has it been determined that the client is agreeable to make the net sale proceeds payable to the registered owner? Typically, a fraudster wants net proceeds payable to third parties. The question of how net proceeds are to be paid upon closing (*only* to the registered owner) should be discussed with client upon opening file.

4) In a sale (of a property other than a condo apartment), can the listing realtor confirm that there was a For Sale sign on the property or, if a private sale, was it a "cooked" sale or was there a For Sale sign on the property with the vendor actually living at the property?

5) Does www.411.ca confirm the reported client address as connecting to one of the client's telephone numbers?

6) Is the "client" only offering a cell phone for contact or are there other residence and business contact phone numbers that can be verified by www.411.ca? A fraudster typically is a "hurried business person" (always on the go) and only wants to be contacted on a cell phone. No sale or refinance matter can be accepted into our office where a client will only provide one phone number being a cell unless the client is also buying.

7) If the transaction is a rushed closing, has the client referred to unhappiness with prior lawyers and, if the job is done efficiently, more business will follow? Fraudsters often like to dangle a "carrot" of future business coming if the innocent duped lawyer acts as an efficient tool of the fraud artist.

8) Is a power of attorney being used and, if so, why? Has the donor of the power of attorney provided a clear copy of a photo ID with a currently dated and signed note that the power of attorney is still valid for the intended purpose and enclosing a contact telephone number? Has the donor of the power of attorney been contacted to verify the facts? Does the signature on the note for the donor (confirming that the power of attorney is still valid) reasonably look like the signature in the power of attorney?

9) If a private sale, was the deposit paid to the seller's lawyer in trust? If so, was the lawyer contacted to verify this? If payable to the vendor direct, watch out! Do not be comforted in a private sale transaction where the deposit was in fact paid to the vendor's lawyer in trust since there have been several fraud situations where this was done by the

fraud artist in order to add legitimacy to the appearance of the transaction. In fraudulent private sales, usually the vendor (impersonating the real owner with a phony ID) and the purchaser (also using a phony ID) are co-conspirators, each using a different innocent duped lawyer as a tool for "purchaser" and for "vendor."

10) If independent legal advice (ILA) is needed for a spouse consent, has it been noted, (as part of the pre-closing processing); telephone the lawyer giving the ILA to confirm he is a lawyer and has given the ILA? There have been cases where the signed consent and the ILA were fraudulent.

11) Is the property mortgage free? In the last six months, has the last security been discharged according to deleted registrations in the parcel register? If so, one might want to confirm with the lender that the discharge was legitimate. If the property is mortgage free, order a copy of the parcel to reveal the deleted instruments so that a clearer picture of recent history of action on title can be revealed.

12) For refinancing, does the parcel register reveal that a non-builder title transfer was registered within the last twelve months for a considerably lower price than the current sold price? If so, how does the client justify the sudden increase? Is the new mortgage lender aware of the sudden increase? Disclosure by fax to the mortgage lender of a recent price increase is now a requirement by most mortgage lenders.

13) Is the client capable of providing all usual documents (including survey, if a non-condo) and property tax bills?

14) Is the property vacant or tenanted?

15) Is the listing broker's first language the same as the vendors?

   NOTE: if suspicions are raised due to at least three items of concern, determine whether the title insurer (if refinancing) should be advised, whether to discuss the matter with another lawyer in the firm, whether to contact the "client" through any other telephone number available from www.411.ca or the white pages of the telephone directory in order to ask a series of questions which might make a fraudster nervous or provide comfort if the client is legitimate. Take extra care when checking photo ID upon sign-up of client and comparing signature on documents to signature on photo ID.

   When a deal becomes suspicious on a sale or refinance, create a SUBFILE called "SUSPICIOUS CIRCUMSTANCES" and insert this form as an analysis checklist and consult S. Shub

   Contact information: Many fraudsters will only provide a cell phone as the means to contact them as they don't want to provide the registered owner's home phone number. A cell number (only) is a red flag, especially if the client refuses to provide a home phone number. Any request to take the documents home is another clear signal to ask more questions.

Appendix 5

Better Business Bureaus

The Better Business Bureaus (BBBs) are non-profit organizations that are supported primarily by local business members in the community.

If you have a particular complaint the BBBs usually request that the complaint be submitted in writing so that an accurate record exists of the dispute. The BBBs will then take up the complaint with the company involved.

If the complaint cannot be resolved in a satisfactory manner through communication with the business, the BBBs may offer an alternative dispute settlement process, such as mediation or arbitration. It is not the role of the BBBs to judge or rate individual products or brands, handle complaints concerning the price of goods or services, handle employer/employee wage disputes, or give legal advice.

Canadian Council of Better Business Bureaus
2 St. Clair Avenue East, Suite 800
Toronto, ON M4T 2T5
Tel.: (416) 644-4936
Fax: (416) 644-4945
Email: ccbbb@canadiancouncilbbb.ca
Website: www.ccbbb.ca

Regional Offices

Alberta
BBB of Southern Alberta
Tel (403) 531-8780
Fax (403) 640-2514
E-mail: info@betterbusinessbureau.ca
Website: www.betterbusinessbureau.ca

BBB Central and Northern Alberta
Tel (780) 482-2341
Toll Free 1-800-232-7298 (across Canada)

Fax: (780) 482-1150
E-mail: info@edmontonbbb.org
Website: www.edmontonbbb.org

British Columbia
BBB of Mainland British Columbia
Tel (604) 682-2711
Fax (604) 681-1544
E-mail: bbbmail@bbbvan.org
Website: www.bbbvan.org

BBB of Vancouver Island
Tel (250) 386-6348
Toll free 1-877-826-4222
Fax (250) 386-2367
E-mail: info@bbbvanisland.org
Website: www.bbbvanisland.org

Manitoba
BBB Manitoba and NorthWestern Ontario
Tel (204) 989-9010
Toll Free 1-800-385-3074
Fax: (204) 989-9016
E-mail: bbbl@mts.net
Website: www.bbbmanitoba.ca

Maritime Region
BBB of the Maritime Provinces
Tel.: (902) 422-6581
Fax: (902) 429-6457
E-mail: bbbmp@bbbmp.ca
Website: www.bbbmp.ca

Newfoundland and Labrador
BBB of Newfoundland and Labrador

Tel (709) 364-2222
Toll Free 1-877-663-2363
Fax (709) 364-2255
E-mail: info@bbbnl.org
Website: www.bbbnl.org

Saskatchewan
BBB of Saskatchewan
Tel (306) 352-7601
Fax (306) 565-6236
E-mail: info@bbbsask.com
Website: www.bbbsask.com

Quebec
BBB of Quebec
Tel (514) 323-1911
Fax (514) 286-2658
E-mail: bbbbec@bbb-bec.com
Website: www.bbb-bec.com

Ontario
BBB of South Central Ontario
Hamilton ON L8N 1A8
Tel (905) 526-1111
Fax (905) 526-1225
E-mail: info@thebbb.ca
Website: www.thebbb.ca

BBB of Greater Toronto Area (GTA)
Tel (519) 579-3080
Toll free 1-800-459-8875
Fax (519) 570-0072
E-mail: info@bbbmwo.ca
Website: www.bbbmwo.ca

BBB Western Ontario
Tel (519) 673-3222
Fax (519) 673-5966
E-mail: info@bbblondon.on.ca
Website: www.bbblondon.on.ca

BBB of Eastern Ontario
Tel (613) 237-4856
Toll Free 1-877-859-8566 (613 Area Code Only)
Fax (613) 237-4878
E-mail: info@ottawa.bbb.org
Website: www.ottawa.bbb.org

BBB of Windsor and South Western Ontario
Tel (519) 258-7222
Fax (519) 258-1198
E-mail: inquiries@windsor.net
Website: www.windsorbbb.com

Appendix 6

Provincial and Territorial Securities Regulators

Alberta
Alberta Securities Commission
Ste. 400 – 300, 5th Avenue SW
Calgary, Alberta T2P 3C4
Tel (403) 297-6454
Toll Free 1-877-355-0585
Fax (403) 297-6156
Website: www.albertasecurities.com
Inquiries: Inquiries@seccom.ab.ca

British Columbia
British Columbia Securities Commission
P.O. Box 10142, Pacific Centre
701 West Georgia Street
Vancouver, British Columbia V7Y 1L2
Tel (604) 899-6500
Toll Free (BC and Alberta) 1-800-373-6393
Fax (604) 899-6506
Website: www.bcsc.bc.ca
Inquiries: inquiries@bcsc.bc.ca

Manitoba
Manitoba Securities Commission
500 – 400 St. Mary Avenue
Winnipeg, Manitoba R3C 4K5
Tel (204) 945-2548
Fax (204) 945-0330
Web site: www.msc.gov.mb.ca
Inquiries: securities@gov.mb.ca

New Brunswick
New Brunswick Securities Commission
85 Charlotte Street, Suite 300
Saint John, NB E2L 2J2
Tel (506) 658-3060

Fax (506) 658-3059
Web site: www.nbsc-cvmnb.ca
Inquiries: information@nbsc-cvmnb.ca

Newfoundland and Labrador
Department of Government Services Consumer &
Commercial Affairs Branch
2nd Floor, West Block Confederation Building
P.O. Box 8700
St. John's, Newfoundland and Labrador A1B 4J6
Tel (709) 729-4189
Fax (709) 729-6187
Website: www.gov.nl.ca/gs

Northwest Territories
Registrar of Securities Legal Registries Division
Department of Justice
Government of the Northwest Territories
1st Floor Stuart M. Hodgson Building
5009 – 49th Street
P.O. Box 1320
Yellowknife, Northwest Territories X1A 2L9
Tel (867) 920-3318
Fax (867) 873-0243
Website: www.justice.gov.nt.ca/SecuritiesRegisty

Nova Scotia
Nova Scotia Securities Commission
Joseph Howe Building
2nd Floor, 1690 Hollis Street
P.O. Box 458
Halifax, Nova Scotia B3J 2P8 / Courier: B3J 3J9
Tel (902) 424-7768
Fax (902) 424-4625
Website: www.gov.ns.ca/nssc

Nunavut
Registrar of Securities Legal Registries Division
Department of Justice
Government of Nunavut
1st Floor, Brown Building
P.O. Box 1000 – Station 570
Iqaluit, Nunavut X0A 0H0
Tel (867) 975-6590
Fax (867) 975-6594

Ontario
Ontario Securities Commission
Box 55, Suite 1903 – 20 Queen Street West
Toronto, Ontario M5H 3S8
Tel (416) 593-8314
Toll Free (Ontario) 1-877-785-1555
Fax (416) 593-8122
Website: www.osc.gov.on.ca
Inquiries: inquiries@osc.gov.on.ca

Prince Edward Island
Securities Office Consumer, Corporate and Insurance
Services Division
Office of the Attorney General
95 Rochford Street, P.O. Box 2000
Charlottetown, Prince Edward Island C1A 7N8
Tel (902) 368-4569
Fax (902) 368-5283
Website: www.gov.pe.ca/securities

Québec
Autorité des marchés financiers
800, Square Victoria, 22e étage
C.P. 246, Tour de la Bourse
Montréal, Québec H4Z 1G3

Tel: Montréal (514) 395-0337
Québec (418) 525-0337
Toll Free 1-877 525-0337
Fax (514) 873-3090
Website: www.lautorite.qc.ca

Saskatchewan
Saskatchewan Financial Services Commission
6th Floor 1919 Saskatchewan Drive
Regina, Saskatchewan S4P 3V7
Tel (306) 787-5645 (Regina)
Fax (306) 787-5899 (Regina)
Website: www.sfsc.gov.sk.ca

Yukon Territory
Registrar of Securities Corporate Affairs and Community
Services
PO Box 2703
Whitehorse, YT Y1A 3C6
Courier: 2130 Second Avenue, 3rd Floor
Whitehorse, YT Y1A 5H6
Tel 867-667-5225
Fax 867-393-6251

Appendix 7

Useful Websites

ABCs of Fraud: http://www.abcfraud.ca/
American Association of Retired Persons:
    http://www.aarp.org/
American Express Canada:
    http://www.americanexpress.com/canada
Anti-Phishing Working Group:
    http://www.antiphishing.org
Canadian Anti-fraud Call Centre:
    http://www.phonebusters.com/
Canadian Association for the 50 Plus: http://www.carp.ca/
Canadian Bankers Association: http://www.cba.ca/
Canadian Council of Better Business Bureaus:
    http://www.canadiancouncilbbb.ca/
Canadian Health Care Anti-fraud Association:
    http://www.chcaa.org/
Canadian Marketing Association:
    www.cmaconsumersense.org
Canadian Securities Administrators:
    http://www.csa-acvm.ca/
Consumer Council of Canada:
    http://www.consumerscouncil.com/
Consumer Measures Committee:
    http://cmcweb.ca/epic/site/
    cmc-cmc.nsf/en/fe00084e.html
Equifax Canada: http://www.equifax.com/EFX_Canada/
FBI: http://www.lookstoogoodtobetrue.com/
**Federal Trade Commission Telemarketing & Telephone
    Services (U.S.)**:
    http://www.ftc.gov/bcp/menus/consumer/phone.shtm
First Canadian Title: http://www.firstcanadiantitle.com
Government of Canada Internet Safety:
    http://safecanada.ca/topic_e.asp?category=3
Heads Up Fraud Prevention Association:
    http://www.heads-up.ca/
Industry Canada:

http://consumer.ic.gc.ca/epic/site/
oca-bc.nsf/en/h_ca02226e.html

Interac Association: http://www.interac.ca

Internet Crime Complaint Center (U.S.):
http://www.ic3.gov/

MasterCard Canada: http://www.mastercard.com/canada/

Microsoft: http://www.microsoft.com/

Mortgage and Title Fraud Protection:
http://www.protectyourtitle.com

National Consumer League: http://www.fraud.org/

Northern Credit Bureaus (Experian):
http://www.creditbureau.ca

OnGuard Online (U.S.): http://www.onguardonline.gov/

Ontario Ministry of Government Services:
http://www.mgs.gov.on.ca/

Ontario Provincial Police: http://www.opp.ca/

RCMP: http://www.rcmp-grc.gc.ca/

Reporting Economic Crime Online: http://www.recol.ca/

Rogers Internet Services: http://www.rogers.com

Service Canada: http://www.servicecanada.gc.ca/en/sc/sin

Symantec Canada (Norton software):
http://www.symantec.com/en/ca/index.jsp

TransUnion: http://www.transunion.ca/

Visa Canada: http://www.visa.ca/en/

Notes

1. "Recent Victim Steps Forward to Advocate for Consumer Awareness of Real Estate Title Fraud." First Canadian Title, 2006. http://www.firstcanadiantitle.com/en/about/news_releases/micro%20site%20launch_June%20506.pdf, accessed June 6, 2007.

2. "Year End Statistics." PhoneBusters, 2007. http://www.phonebusters.com/english/documents/Yearlyen0001_000.pdf, accessed June 6, 2007.

3. "Thieves are cashing in on debit cards." Paul Dalby, Toronto Star, 8 March 2007, http://www.thestar.com/Special/article/188460, accessed June 6, 2007.

4. "Fraud and Security." Canadian Bankers Association, 2007. http://www.cba.ca/en/ViewDocument.asp?fl=3&sl=308&tl=310&docid=546, accessed June 6, 2007.

5. "Credit Card Fraud." AARP, 2007. http://www.aarp.org/money/wise_consumer/scams/a2002-10-01-Frauds CreditCards.html, accessed June 6, 2007.

6. "Thieves are cashing in on debit cards." Paul Dalby, Toronto Star, 8 March 2007, http://www.thestar.com/Special/article/188460, accessed June 6, 2007.

7. "Credit Card Fraud." AARP, 2007. http://www.aarp.org/money/wise_consumer/scams/a2002-10-01-FraudsCreditCards.html, accessed June 6, 2007.

8. "How Identity Theft Strikes." Equifax, 2007. http://www.equifax.com/credit-information/identity-

theft, accessed June 6, 2007.

9. "Cybercrime Stories." Symantec Corporation, 2007. http://www.symantec.com/avcenter/cybercrime/index_pa ge4_story2.html, accessed June 6, 2007.

10. "Cybercrime Stories." Symantec Corporation, 2007. http://www.symantec.com/avcenter/cybercrime/index_pa ge4_story2.html, accessed June 6, 2007.

11. "Stopping Spam: Creating a Stronger, Safer Internet." Industry Canada, 2005. http://e-com.ic.gc.ca/epic/site/ecic-ceac.nsf/en/gv00321e.html, accessed June 6, 2007.

12. "Wireless Security." OnGuard Online, 2007. http://www.onguardonline.gov/wireless.html, accessed June 6, 2007.

13. "Straight talk parent to parent." Heads Up Fraud Prevention, 2007. http://www.heads-up.ca/hottips/Tips/Straight%20talk%20parent%20to%20parent.pdf, accessed June 6, 2007.

14. "Cybercrime Stories." Symantec Corporation, 2007. http://www.symantec.com/avcenter/cybercrime/index_pa ge4_story4.html, accessed June 6, 2007.

15. "Spyware." OnGuard Online, 2007. http://www.onguard online.gov/spyware.html, accessed June 6, 2007.

16. "Signs of viruses: Are you infected?" Microsoft Corporation, 20 September 2006. http://www.microsoft.com/protect/computer/viruses/indicators.mspx, accessed June 6, 2007.

17. "Mortgage fraud hits $1.5b a year." Mario Toneguzzi, Calgary Herald, 18 March 2006. http://www.protecty-ourtitle.com/images/pdf/CalgaryHerald.pdf, accessed June 6, 2007.

18. "When a house is not a home." Harold Levy, Toronto Star, 26 August 2006. http://www.thestar.com/printArti-cle/144240, accessed June 6, 2007.

19. "First Canadian Title 2006 Annual Report." First Canadian Title, 2006. http://www.firstcanadiantitle. com/en/about/annual_report/WEB_Eng_2006_Annual-Report.pdf, accessed June 6, 2007.

20. "Consumer Information on Real Estate Fraud." Canadian Association of Accredited Mortgage Professionals, 2007. http://www.caamp.org/FRAUD_INTRO.htm, accessed June 6, 2007.

21. "Tips to Avoid Nigerian or '419' Fraud." LooksToo-GoodToBeTrue.com, 2007. http://www.lookstoogoodto-betrue.com/pop/fin3.aspx, accessed June 6, 2007.

22. "OSC Warns Investors to Beware of Phantom Regulators." Ontario Securities Commission, 2007. http://www. osc.gov.on.ca/Investor/Alert/ia_20050830_phantom-reg-ulators.jsp, accessed June 6, 2007.

23. "Investor Watch: Advertisements promoting investment opportunities." Canadian Securities Administrators, 2006. https://www.csa-acvm.ca/html_CSA/invinfo_ad_pro-moting.html, accessed June 6, 2007.

24. "What is Deceptive Telemarketing?" PhoneBusters, 2007. http://www.phonebusters.com/english/fraudpre-

vention_backgrounder.html, accessed June 6, 2007.

25. "Toll Free Telephone Number Scams." Federal Trade Commission, 1997. http://www.ftc.gov/bcp/conline/ pubs/tmarkg/tollfree.shtm, accessed June 6, 2007.

26. "RCMP probe U.S. senior scams." Charles Duhigg, New York Times, 21 May 2007. http://www.thestar.com/article/216075, accessed June 6, 2006.

27. "Seniors as victims of crime." Statistics Canada, 2007. http://www.statcan.ca/english/research/85F0033MIE/85F 0033MIE2007014.htm, accessed June 6, 2007.

28. "Respecting Our Elders: A Statewide Action Plan To Combat Senior Fraud." Office of the Colorado Attorney General, 1999. http://www.ago.state.co.us/consprot/SE-NIORFRAUDRPT.pdf, accessed June 6, 2007.

29. "Wise Owls." Heads Up Fraud Prevention Association, 2007. http://www.heads-up.ca/wise_owls.htm, accessed June 6, 2007.

30. "Providing Assistance to Senior Fraud Victims." Crimes of Persuasion, 2000. http://www.crimes-of-persuasion.com/Crimes/Telemarketing/Outbound/Major/ Sweepstakes/assistance.htm, accessed June 6, 2007.

31. "Senior Beware: Avoiding Con Artist Schemes." Senior Series: Ohio State University Extension and Ohio Aging Network, 2007. http://ohioline.osu.edu/ss-fact/0121.html, accessed June 6, 2007.

32. "Charitable Donations: Give or Take?" Federal Trade Commission, 2003. http://www.ftc.gov/bcp/conline

/pubs/tmarkg/charity.shtm, accessed June 6, 2007.

33. "Faith-Based Investment Scams on the Rise." Better Business Bureau, 2001. http://www.bbb.org/alerts/article.asp?id=289, accessed June 6, 2007.

34. "Canada, Mexico and the United States combat weight-loss fraud." Health Canada, 2005. http://www.hc-sc.gc.ca/ahc-asc/media/nr-cp/2005/2005_113_e.html, accessed June 6, 2007.

35. "Criminal Charges Laid in Cancer Treatment Scam Following Competition Bureau Investigation." Competition Bureau Canada, 2 August 2005. http://www.competition-bureau.gc.ca/internet/index.cfm?itemid=1928, accessed June 6, 2007.

References

Chapter 1: Identity Theft

"Coping with Identity Theft: Reducing the Risk of Fraud." Privacy Rights Clearinghouse, 2007. http://www.privacyrights.org/fs/fs17-it.htm, accessed June 6, 2007.

"Deadline for expiry of Social Insurance Numbers beginning with 9." Human Resources and Social Development Canada, 2004. http://www.hrsdc.gc.ca/en/cs/comm/sd/news/2004/040402.shtml, accessed June 6, 2007.

"Identity Theft: Who's Using Your Name?" Office of the Information and Privacy Commissioner/Ontario, 1997. http://www.ipc.on.ca/images/Resources/idtheft-e.pdf, accessed June 6, 2007.

"Lost, stolen, damaged, destroyed or inaccessible passport." Passport Canada, 2007. http://www.ppt.gc.ca/can/lost_stolen.aspx?lang=e, accessed June 6, 2007.

"Marine stumbles on stolen ID." *Sentinel Reporter*. 30 March 2007. http://www.cumberlink.com/articles/2007/03/30/news/news667.prt, accessed June 6, 2007.

"Ottawa police break up major identity theft ring." CBC News, 9 March 2006. http://www.cbc.ca/canada/story/2006/03/09/20060309-idtheft.html, accessed June 6, 2007.

"Social Insurance Number." Service Canada, 2007. http://www.servicecanada.gc.ca/en/sc/sin, accessed June 6, 2007.

"A stolen life: Identity theft nightmare." Lori Culbert. Vancouver Sun, 2006. https://www.cs.ubc.ca/local/computing/practices/documents/IdentityTheft.pdf, accessed June 6, 2007.

Chapter 2: Debit and Credit Card Fraud

"Avoiding Credit and Charge Card Fraud." Federal Trade Commission, 1997. http://www.ftc.gov/bcp/conline/pubs/credit/cards.htm, accessed June 6, 2007.

Hamadi, Rob. *Identity Theft: What Is It, How to Prevent It and What to Do If It Happens to You.* London, England: Fusion Press, 2004.

"Identity Theft." Canadian Bankers Association, 2007. http://www.cba.ca/en/viewdocument.asp?fl=3&sl=308&tl=311&docid=690, accessed June 6, 2007.

"Ottawa police break up major identity theft ring." CBC News, 9 March 2006. http://www.cbc.ca/canada/story/2006/03/09/20060309-idtheft.html, accessed June 6, 2007.

"Security." Interac, Inc., 2007. http://www.interac.ca/en_n1_40_security.html, accessed June 6, 2007.

Chapter 3: Credit Reports

"Fraud and Identity Theft." TransUnion, 2007. http://www.transunion.ca/ca/personal/fraudidentity theft_en.page, accessed June 6, 2007.

Chapter 4: Internet and E-Mail Fraud

"Detect and Defend against E-Mail Fraud." Rogers Communications, Inc., 2007. http://www.shoprogers.com/store/cable/email_fraud.asp, accessed June 6, 2007.

"Don't Get Taken to the Bank – Protect Your ATM and Debit Cards." Better Business Bureau, 2004. http://www.bbb.org/Alerts/article.asp?ID=307, accessed June 6, 2007.

"FBI Says Web 'Spoofing' Scams are a Growing Problem." Federal Bureau of Investigation, 2003. http://www.fbi.gov/pressrel/pressrel03/spoofing072103.htm, accessed June 6, 2007.

"For Consumers: Every Canadian is a consumer." Competition Bureau Canada, 2007. http://www.competitionbureau.gc.ca/internet/index.cfm?itemID=17&lg=e, accessed June 6, 2007.

"How Not to Get Hooked by a 'Phishing' Scam." Federal Trade Commission, 2006. http://www.ftc.gov/bcp/edu/pubs/consumer/alerts/alt127.shtm, accessed June 6, 2007.

"Identity Theft – A Primer." Office of the Privacy Commissioner of Canada, 2007. http://www.privcom.gc.ca/id/primer_e.asp, accessed June 6, 2007.

"Phishing and Spoofing." LooksTooGoodToBeTrue.com, 2007. http://www.lookstoogoodtobetrue.com/fraudtypes/phishing.aspx, accessed June 6, 2007.

"Stop – Think – Click: 7 Practices for Safer Computing." OnGuard Online, 2005. http://onguardonline.gov/stopthinkclick.html, accessed June 6, 2007.

"Senior Beware: Avoiding Con Artist Schemes." Senior Series: Ohio State University Extension and Ohio Aging Network, 2007. http://ohioline.osu.edu/ss-fact/0121.html, accessed June 6, 2007.

"Spam." LooksTooGoodToBeTrue.com, 2007. http://www.lookstoogoodtobetrue.com/fraudtypes/spam.aspx, accessed June 6, 2007.

"A stolen life: Identity theft nightmare." Lori Culbert. Vancouver Sun, 2006. https://www.cs.ubc.ca/local/computing/practices/documents/IdentityTheft.pdf, accessed June 6, 2007.

Chapter 7: Telephone Fraud

"809 Area Code Scam." Snopes.com, 2005. http://www.snopes.com/fraud/telephone/809.asp, accessed June 6, 2007.

Chapter 8: Fraud against Seniors

"Avoiding Investment Fraud." National Crime Prevention

Council, 2007. http://www.ncpc.org/cms/cms-upload/ncpc/file/3671-Avoid%20Investment%20Fraud.pdf, accessed June 6, 2007.

"Charitable Giving Done Wisely." National Crime Prevention Council, 2007. http://www.ncpc.org/cms/cms-upload/ ncpc/File/charity%20fraud.pdf, accessed June 6, 2007.

"Seniors and Telemarketing Fraud 101." National Crime Prevention Council, 2006. http://www.ncpc.org/ncpc_cms/ SenFraud_rev4.pdf, accessed June 6, 2007.

"Schemes, Scams & Cons." Heads Up Fraud Prevention Association, 2007. http://www.heads-up.ca/schemes.htm, accessed June 6, 2007.

"'Urgent and Confidential'—The Nigerian Letter Scam." National Crime Prevention Council, 2007. http://www.ncpc.org/cms/cms-upload/ncpc/File/Nigerian%20Scam.pdf, accessed June 6, 2007.

Chapter 9: Other Fraud

"Be an informed donor." Canada Revenue Agency, 2005. http://www.cra-arc.gc.ca/newsroom/factsheets/ 2005/nov/fs051110-3-e.html, accessed June 6, 2007.

"Canada Mexico and the United States combat weight-loss fraud." Health Canada, 2005. http://www.hc-sc.gc.ca/ahc-asc/media/nr-cp/2005/2005_113_e.html, accessed June 6, 2007.

"Charity Checklist." Ottawa Police Service, 2007. http://www.ottawapolice.ca/en/serving_ottawa/support_units/fraud_charity_checklist.cfm, accessed June 6, 2007.

Bibliography

Drake, Elizabeth. *50 Plus One Tips to Preventing Identity Theft*, Chicago: Encouragement Press, LLC, 2007.

Mcwaters, Graham, and Winthrop Sheldon. *The Canadian Student Financial Survival Guide*, Toronto: Insomniac Press, 2005.

Waite, Melanie. *Personal Information and Scams Protection: A Canadian Practical Guide*, Ottawa: RCMP, 2007.

Index

Contributing Author

Connie Bird is a senior account manager with a national insurer. She has twenty-five years of experience in retail banking, the securities industry, and, most recently, educating professionals involved in the real estate industry from lawyers to lenders to mortgage brokers. Connie is also a professional workshop presenter and keynote speaker. Her topics include persuasion, identity theft, and fraud.

Connie assisted with all aspects of the book with special emphasis on the chapters covering identity theft, and mortgage and title fraud. Her thorough knowledge of these areas made the book more complete. We thank Connie for her expertise and contributions.

Acknowledgements

The authors of this book would like to acknowledge and thank Stephen H. Shub, LL.B., Barrister, Solicitor, and Notary for his great contribution to the Real Estate Lawyer Checklist in the appendix. This is a must-read for all lawyers who practice real estate law. It is an interesting piece for the consumer as it shows the amount of work the lawyer performs to protect real estate and mortgage transactions from fraudsters.

We would also like to thank the following four executives from First Canadian Title for their contribution to the chapter on mortgage and title fraud: Susan Leslie, Ivo Winter, Lorne Shuman, and Mary De Sousa. Their knowledge and experiences in this area is outstanding and assisted us in outlining the true story behind this type of fraud.